For Faith,

with love,

Carolyn

April 1986

An Elephant for Muthu

CAROLYN SLOAN

THE BODLEY HEAD
LONDON

British Library Cataloguing in Publication Data
Sloan, Carolyn
An elephant for Muthu.
I. Title
823'.914 [J] PZ7
ISBN 0–370–30897–2

Copyright © Carolyn Sloan 1986
Phototypeset by Wyvern Typesetting Ltd, Bristol
Printed in Finland for
The Bodley Head Ltd
30 Bedford Square, London WC1B 3RP
by Werner Söderström Oy
First published 1986

1

"You're just a wild jungle boy, aren't you? Like a monkey. No, not as clever as a monkey. Well?" Palani waited for Muthu to get angry, but he didn't. He climbed further up the stockade to get closer to the new elephant, smiling to himself. Palani would never understand that he *liked* being called a jungle boy. He knew a lot about the jungle, he was a good tracker. Yes, he could even move like a monkey—very nearly.

"So?" Muthu said placidly.

"So? That's all? Why don't you argue with me?"

"If you want to argue with monkeys there are plenty in those trees."

"Don't cheek me like that! I'm older than you, remember."

Muthu could never forget that Palani was older. Palani would have his own elephant long before Muthu had his. He wished his bullying cousin would go away and leave him with the new elephant. He'd rather talk to an elephant any time, especially to this one because he had come from the wild, and Muthu had only been close to elephants born in the camp before.

"He'll grow into a fine tusker," Muthu said admiringly. "You can see the tips already, look!"

"Elephants! You never think of anything but elephants. You never think of getting away from here and doing something interesting."

"No," said Muthu because he didn't. He had been born in the elephant camp. His father was a mahout and he just dreamed of the day he had his own elephant and was on the way to being a mahout too. He supposed that one day he would get married and have lots of children, it would be expected. He might even like the children. But his elephant would be the most special thing in his life. It would be the best elephant in the whole of India. He got closer to the new one and started to talk to him in a monotonous, soothing chant. Palani stretched out on the top timber of the stockade and lit a beedie.

"Stop making that irritating noise," he said.

"He has to learn to get used to us, Rengan said so."

"Learn? From you?" Palani snorted. "I tell you what I learned last evening in the bazaar. They were talking of cutting the new road."

"They are always talking, never cutting," said Muthu. "It won't come, the new road. I hope it doesn't."

"But don't you see? If the road came here then maybe there would be a bus as well. Maybe once, maybe twice each week! We could get away from here like they do at the big camp at Theppakkadu. The camp children would go to school!"

Muthu could see nothing to get excited about. "Why should they go to school?" he said vaguely.

"To learn to read things on papers. To write things, of course. I have always wanted to go to school."

Muthu thought about it. He'd seen people writing things down, important people, like the Range Officer, who came in jeeps. They asked the elephant men questions about the elephants, and about stores and timber... and then they wrote the things they said down and there was always a lot of arguing about whether the things that were written down were the things the men had said. In the end they agreed and the little tin of blue stuff was brought out for the elephant men to put their thumb-prints on the papers. Muthu's father's thumb would be blue all day and Muthu kept asking him to show it to him because it was an interesting colour that didn't happen naturally in the jungle. Muthu longed for the day when he would put his thumb in the blue tin too to show that he was an elephant man.

"You're dreaming. Not listening," said Palani crossly. Muthu dragged his mind back to his cousin. "Why do you want to do reading and writing when there's the blue tin?" he said.

"Because, elephant-boy, I would go to a city and get a Government job. In an *office*," he said with exaggerated patience. "In an office you do things with papers and you send them here and there. In a proper office building made of . . . stones, I think, yes! And glass in the windows you can see through. And . . . a fan turning over my head to keep me cool. I have been to Mysore, I know how these things are. I would just have to clap my hands like *this*! And a boy—a stupid one like you—would bring me a glass of tea."

Muthu stared in amazement and started to laugh.

"It isn't funny, it's true. In a Government office I would make lots of rupees to spend in the bazaar. A proper one, not like here, with electric lights hanging on wires . . . and stalls with clothes already made, clothes like the film stars wear in Bombay . . ." He stopped suddenly and spat angrily, "When the road comes, we will both be too old to go to school."

"They don't teach you how to teach elephants in schools, though, do they?" Muthu said, puzzling about it.

"Of course they don't. Who wants to teach stupid elephants?"

"They're not stupid!" said Muthu, losing his temper. "They're not, they're . . ."

"Stop squealing like a little pig. You're not worth talking to. I shall go and find my friends in the bazaar." He swung himself down from the stockade and strode off arrogantly towards the bazaar path. Muthu watched him go and thought, wistfully, how nice it would be if he never came back. It was quiet in the lazy heat of the afternoon. The great stands of bamboo by the river could scarcely be bothered to rustle. Two elephants off work swayed in the shade, dozing on their feet. Some of the old people were asleep, their string beds pulled out of the stuffy low shacks and under the feathery casurina trees. Only the voices of women gossiping over their washing in the river broke the stillness, that and the slap of wet clothes on the rocks. Muthu looked round the camp with a feeling of great contentment. It was all clean and tidy, ready for the elephants when they came back from work. Soon Rengan would come and unlock the stores and weigh out their evening rations. It was a good place to be. Palani was crazy not to see that. It was deep in the jungle many miles from the big camp at Theppakkadu which was on the main road from Mysore up into the distant Nilgiris Hills. Years before it had just been a temporary logging camp, but it was in such a good place on a bend in the river that the Range Officer had made it a permanent camp. Muthu liked it, for its wildness, better than the big camp. There were only twenty working elephants and some youngsters in training, their mahouts, their kavadis and the men's families. Their bamboo huts ran along one edge of the camp like a fringe. The only other buildings were the vast and solid elephant stockades and the thatched platform which was the elephants' kitchen. The rest was a clearing, the grass burnt dry with the sun, and the red earth showing through like a threadbare carpet. But the jungle around was green from the recent rains, and because the river was there, looping round the camp like two separate rivers. On one side it was grassy with sloping sand banks and a shallow pool where the baby elephants liked to play. On the other side it was harsher, and plunged dramatically through boulders as big and as grey as the elephants themselves. There was no bamboo growing on that side, but tough, gaunt trees whose roots, coiling like rat snakes, reached down to the water. The trees perched on their roots as though they were trying to climb out of the river and run away.

Meenakshi was coming to the river on the sandy side, with a load of fresh bamboo and grass. The young kavadi on her neck wiggled his toes behind her ears, telling her what to do, as if she needed telling. She was patchy pink with age now and Muthu treated her rather like his grandmother, with affection and deep respect. But he loved her specially as an elephant for her peculiar, elderly gait, her solemn dignity and her tattered second-hand ears. She stepped delicately into the river and then stopped to take a drink, stretching her trunk to its full length to reach the clear water that had not been muddied by her feet. Muthu watched her take her little detour from the beaten track so she would not have to pass the place where her old mahout had dropped dead at her feet. She had not understood that and she had been dangerous then. Not even her kavadi could get close to her. She just stood over the body for two days, until it began to rot. Muthu had been smaller then and he had gone and hidden in the darkest corner of his hut because the old elephant breaking her great heart with grief was more than he could bear to watch. Vishnu, the vet from Theppakkadu, had come, and gone away again because there was nothing he could do. Muthu had run after him—he squirmed with embarrassment to think of it now—crying "You are the doctor, you have to help her," and his mother had been angry because Vishnu was a clever and important man who had been to Bombay, and Muthu was just an elephant man's son.

Meenakshi had gone away, suddenly, into the jungle and they had quickly burned the mahout's body. The elephant men said she had gone away to die, but weeks later she ambled back into the camp as if she had just had a holiday. The vet had come to see her, and he had spoken especially to Muthu, who had nearly burst with pride. "You see Muthuswamy..." Yes! He even knew his name! "You see she has got over her sorrow now?" But he spoiled her as much as anyone else because he knew she had not got over it and she never would.

The wild young elephant in the stockade was fidgeting nervously. Muthu climbed down the outside until he was close to his head. He found a long sliver of bamboo and pushed it through the timbers so that it rasped on the elephant's wrinkled skin. The elephant kept very still and taut, but did not move away. It was dangerous, Muthu knew that. With one quick movement he could be pulled into the stockade and kneed to the ground. His father or Rengan would be angry if they knew. But they weren't there.

"It's all right," he said gently. "You can trust me. It's a good place, your home now. See how the other elephants like it? Did you see Meenakshi coming with your food for the night? Soon Rengan will open the cookhouse and they will make you a big cake. And you will have sugar cane and coconuts. You're listening to me, aren't you, that's good." The elephant was uncertain, but Muthu thought he was calmed by his voice and the rhythmic rubbing of the stick. His little wise eyes fastened on Muthu briefly and then slid away again, gazing short-sightedly, but with a terrible longing, through the bars of his prison, out into the jungle where he had been born and lived free.

"Don't do that!" Muthu said, and his voice was rough-edged because he felt the animal's longing as if it were his own. The elephant drew back suspiciously. Muthu started again, soothingly. "You are afraid of people and that makes you angry, but it is only because you are wild and you don't know them. But we know elephants. We have always known elephants. Believe me, it is true. When I was a baby—that's like a new-born calf, you understand—who did I meet first? Before my aunts and uncles even? Lakshmi, my father's elephant. They have been together, my father and Lakshmi, for nearly thirty years. They will go on working together for another thirty years. What do you think of that? And when I was still a small calf, still on four legs, like you, I played under Lakshmi's feet. I could hardly reach above her toe-nails. But she looked after me. When I crawled away she pulled me back with her trunk, and when I was naughty she slapped me with it!" Muthu didn't really remember it, he remembered his mother telling him about it later. "I was never afraid for you, why should I be? And when you could walk you were always wanting to do things for elephants." He remembered that. Trying to drag a bucket of water as big as himself up from the river. Reaching up to rub a sore on Lakshmi's leg. And his mother saying—"Oh that Muthu! He will do anything for Lakshmi. But where is he when *I* want something done?" But she had laughed because it did not matter. She had four girls to help her already, but Muthu, her first son, he would be a mahout one day!

"One day," said Muthu dreamily. "I wish it was today and you were my elephant! Your kavadi will come soon, Rajiv, he's working many days away now—but when he hears about you he will fly like the god of the wind to get back here. He will tame you and when you lose your wild spirit you'll be like the others. Then he will teach you many things and when you are big enough and clever enough—not for many years yet—then you will go to work and he will be made mahout. And there will be another kavadi to bath you and cook your food and hook the chains when you are dragging timber." The elephant swayed and rubbed one of his back legs against the other. There was still a mark where the capture rope had been. "Why did you struggle so?" Muthu said indignantly. "No one wanted to hurt you. *We* didn't dig the pit you fell into, bad people did that. But *you* fell into it, why did you? *Our* elephants never fall into pits because their mahouts show them where they are. It's good to be a camp elephant, the others are happy." The elephant gave him a look of such hatred that Muthu winced, because he, Muthu, was the enemy and he did not want to be. "All right," he said reasonably, "who brought you here? Elephants, your own kind, did, not us! My father's Lakshmi and Geeva, remember? Didn't they press against you so that you couldn't kick and run? Didn't they flap their ears over your eyes so that you didn't see my father slip down and put the rope on your foot? And why was it that you were . . ." Muthu stopped himself. He was going to say why were you alone? Wild elephants look after each other, they look after young ones especially, but they didn't look after you. Why did your herd leave you there alone?

The herd had not meant to leave him. The bang and

the fire had panicked them into a stampede, and when it was over the leader had had to make a decision which troubled her great mother's heart. The safety of the whole herd was now threatened, she must lead them away at once, leaving behind a young male who would one day become a fine tusker, and a mother with her first calf who had gone the wrong way.

They had been greedy. A small village had grown up on the elephants' traditional route. Most years they went round it, but this year the villagers' crops had grown, and there was a tempting plantation of ripening bananas. The leader rested the herd during the day, and when the hot land wind blew the broad banana leaves flapped their ragged edges and wafted the warm fruity smell to them. The baby of the herd was impatient. He wanted to go after the smell right away and had to be slapped back. His mother made it clear that there was danger, but it was not a danger he had met before: people.

In the moonlight the herd moved towards the banana plantation and the leading elephants pushed the fences away as if they were cobwebs. Soon they were tearing down the trees and there was a contented squelching, munching and happy grunting noise. And then the bang. It came out of the night with no warning. The little elephant felt his mother's vast weight shudder with shock and she let out a terrible gurgling squeal. The herd gathered round the leader and she made a quick decision; she tucked her trunk into her mouth out of harm's way and charged on towards the village, the herd stampeding behind her. Bamboo huts were trampled flat, a woman screamed, a kerosene lamp overturned and then there were flames flaring, roaring, turning the sky orange.

The baby elephant struggled to keep up with his mother as she crashed, dazed and crazed, through the jungle. A young male followed them. In the confusion they had rushed the wrong way; the herd was moving off in the opposite direction and the fire blazed between them. The next day they were miles apart and the young elephant had disappeared. The baby elephant was bewildered. Where was the friendly shuffling herd who had always been there? For the whole of his one and a half years the great tree-trunk legs had towered above him. The whispering feet had stopped on the day that he was born, gathered round on his first night to protect him from the jungle, moved slowly until he could keep up with them. But now they had gone and he was alone with his mother. A strange mother now, who did not play with him or slap him and pull him back when he strayed. And when he went to her for milk and comfort she had little of either to give him. They no longer went into the deep jungle where she used to pull down branches for him to eat the juicy leaves. He did not realise that she couldn't do that any more. The bang that had frightened them all had been a blunderbuss and its load of rusty nails had hit her trunk. At first she just felt dazed and stung, but each day her wounds became more infected and they spread until her trunk was swollen and stiff. Each day it became more painful; she became more helpless. They went, usually at night, near villages where she could kick the crops out of the ground and find food for her baby. But the human smell near villages made her restless and edgy.

Once when they were out during the day they found a man's brass tiffin carrier and his head-cloth hanging from a tree. She went into a wild rage, flung the tiffin carrier into the distance and attacked the headcloth, stamping and tearing it and squealing with pain and rage. The man had been cutting firewood nearby, he tried to climb into a tree but she pulled him down. The baby trotted round squealing with alarm as she trumpeted her rage and knelt heavily on him. Then silence. When she got up and walked away there was no man. Just a patch of blood drying in the sun and shattered bones and shreds of cloth ground into the earth.

2

The sun moving behind the peepul tree told Muthu it was four o'clock and that deep in the jungle the elephants would be packing up and getting ready to come back. They were perfect timekeepers and knew that they started work at half past eight in the morning, they stopped for an hour in the heat of the day, and they packed up at four o'clock. No one could make them work a moment's overtime. They would be picking up their ropes and chains now to carry home, kneeling for their mahouts and kavadis to climb up. The camp prepared for them; they would be hot and tired and ready for their baths. Hungry for their special rations, looking forward to the evening when they would be left to roam the jungle and munch their way through more than three hundred kilos of fresh fodder until the kavadis collected them again at five o'clock the next morning.

Muthu dragged himself away from the new elephant and went to help Rengan weigh out the horsegram and ragi for the elephants' cakes, their salt and jaggery rations. Each elephant had its own diet depending on its size and health. There was sugar cane for the young calves and rice and coconuts for mother elephants and those expecting calves. The smoke from the cookhouse fires mingled with the still-hot musty air. Rengan sweated and swore over the cooking pots.

"Ay! Palani, Muthu, where are you, idle fellows? There is not enough water, where have you been, sleeping under a tree?"

"You told us to stay near the new elephant," said Muthu quietly.

"So you slept behind the stockade instead then? You didn't mend those ropes?"

"No," said Muthu. Palani had been told to do that. Muthu supposed he would be blamed once again for something Palani had failed to do.

"There is dung not cleared, just thrown into the lantana bushes. You know elephants don't eat where ..."

"I know," said Muthu hotly because he knew very well what the elephants liked and did not like. It was Palani again.

"Get some water then," Rengan said more kindly. "I suppose that Palani is idling in the bazaar again, is he?"

"He wouldn't do that," said Muthu as unconvincingly as he could.

Muthu was hauling heavy buckets of water up from the river when he realised that Palani was leaning against a tree watching him. He dropped the buckets angrily. "You! Standing there. Help me get the water."

"You don't tell me what to do, monkey-brat," Palani said slowly.

"Rengan was asking for you."

"You told him where I was, did you, crawler? Did you?"

"I said you would not have gone to the bazaar."

"Why did you say 'bazaar' at all?"

"He's angry with *me*! It's always me, always."

"You *told* him!" Palani grasped Muthu by his hair and shook him like a dog shaking a bandycoot. His eyes burned with anger but he spoke in a menacingly calm voice. "Tell Rengan I didn't go to the bazaar. But I shall go and I shall bring my friends back. You remember them, Muthu?"

"No!" Muthu squeaked, remembering them vividly. "Palani, don't do that . . ."

"We'll send you swimming again inside the bat cave, Muthuswamy. In the dark cave, where the bats cling onto your hair . . . in the dark, where the king cobra waits . . . at the end . . ."

"I'll tell Rengan you have gone grass cutting . . . that you'll come soon."

"Yes. And then go and cut some grass for me. Do that."

Muthu's head felt raw where Palani had tugged at his hair. He went back to the river and poured water over it, trying to wash away the pain and his loathing for Palani at the same time. The distant, brassy dongs of the returning elephants' bells broke into his anger, and he hurried back to camp to see the best sight of the day. The line of homecoming elephants were cut out on a ridge against the sky like a temple carving. He saw at once that something was wrong. Lakshmi, unusually, was leading and Chinoo, his father's kavadi, was slumped across her neck, his headcloth covering his head. A group of people gathered, knowing instinctively, as Muthu had done, that something was wrong. Accidents happened sometimes far away at the logging sites. Muthu and Chinoo's wife, her sari over her head, went forward hesitantly to meet them.

"Chinoo has fever, it is nothing more," Muthu's father called out reassuringly. In the camp Lakshmi knelt and the floppy, groaning Chinoo was carried to his hut.

"He is very sick," Chinoo's wife called over her shoulder. "Why didn't you bring him back sooner?" She was angry with worry or she would not have spoken out at his mahout.

"He will be all right," Muthu's father shouted back. He climbed down on Lakshmi's bent leg and Muthu went forward to take her rope and chain from her mouth.

"Wait, Muthu!" his father said sharply. He was searching round for someone to take Lakshmi down to the river for her evening bath.

"I will take her," said Muthu stoutly. His father

frowned. He would happily bath Lakshmi himself, but there was a chain of importance in the camp that ruled who was seen to be doing which job.

"Call Palani."

"He is not here," Muthu said. "But I am." His father gave in and grinned. Muthu scrambled onto Lakshmi's spread leg and she moved, sensing him like a spider, making it easier for him to climb on to her neck. She could see the joke. She told her mahout so with her little piggy amused eyes. So! This little one thinks he can bath me all by himself! Let us see! She lumbered solemnly down the sandy bank to the river and waited while Muthu unhooked her bell chain and the working chain from her back leg. Then he called shrilly to her and she stepped daintily into the water on her soft, soup-plate feet. With a great sigh of contentment she lay down in the river, sending ripples across to the other side. Her head sank, another ripple, the grey-pink tip of her trunk appeared like a snorkel. Muthu doubled up his dhoti and knotted it—no matter that the water came up to his armpits and sometimes he had to tread water. He took a piece of rough jack-fruit skin from a coil of tree root that was used as an elephants' bath rack and started to scrub Lakshmi vigorously. He scrambled along her leg precariously to reach into her wrinkles and dislodge the twigs in the folds of her neck. He turned over the flap of her ear to scrub the pink side, searching out bugs and ticks that had burrowed in during the day and could cause bad sores later on. His arms ached with the strain, down his neck and his back. He sat on Lakshmi's head, puffed, and then shouted the 'turn over' command into her ear. Lakshmi coiled her trunk like a river snake and then she arched it and aimed such an accurate and powerful jet of water at Muthu that he fell into the river. He came up spluttering and shaking his fist. "Lakshmi," he gasped, "when I am mahout, you will not dare play such tricks on me!" There was a shaking figure on the bank—his father helpless with laughter at his jokey elephant and his serious son.

"You've been there all the time!" Muthu said indignantly as his father plunged into the river and started to scrub Lakshmi all over again. When he told her to turn over she rose slowly with water cascading from her shoulders and flopped back into the river, sending out new waves of ripples that made Muthu stagger. She came out at last, cooled and refreshed, and blew hot sand over her back to dry off. Muthu wanted to be the one to give her her evening rations, to put on her hobble chain and send her off into the jungle for the night. But his mother was calling to him. She was sitting at the entrance to their hut inspecting one of his sisters' heads and oiling her hair.

"Now you have done kavadi's work you can go to the bazaar for me," she said. Muthu groaned, but quietly. He hated going to the bazaar in case Palani and his friends were there. They always picked on him, and he felt uncomfortable there. His mother wanted rice and oil. He sighed and went into the hut to find the hessian bag and the money, which she kept knotted in a strip of old sari stuffed into the thatch. It was a big hut—Muthu's father being a mahout—with two rooms and a veranda where his mother lit the cooking fire. It creaked in the dry weather and smelt musty, but when the big rains came they sometimes swept a tide of orange mud and water right through, and it smelt of mildew and mushrooms. Muthu liked it, he liked the feel of the smooth, polished cow dung floor under his feet. He found the money and disturbed a lizard lurking in the thatch.

"Take a torch, Muthu," his mother called. "It will be dark before you get back."

Muthu took his time getting to the bazaar. The track was just wide enough for a jeep and it went from steamy jungle where the trees were close together and choked with creepers, on through teak forests, brown and crinkly underfoot, and then spread out into open grasslands, with just an odd spikey tree or mound of rock appearing unexpectedly.

The sun was low in the special hour before darkness came, suddenly as it did there, with no twilight. The colours changed, became more important in this special hour. Dusty, sandy shades glowed warm orange, the greens were very pure, dark greens, and the great far bulk of the Nilgiris

Hills went through every shade of blue and grey and purple until they were mere black outlines on the sky, and then were gone. Muthu liked this time of day. The jungle was so busy now the heat had gone. He could sense night creatures all around him getting ready to come out for their night's hunting as the day creatures took a last drink at the river before they retired. The birds were already swooping and wheeling and arguing overhead.

Muthu met the herd boys from the camp bringing the buffalo back from their grazing grounds. No, they said, they had not seen Palani and they didn't want to. He bullied them too and stole milk, but they dare not tell anyone. By the time Muthu got to the bazaar they were lighting the kerosene lamps over the stalls. A new holy man had arrived and fitted himself, like an ancient statue, into a corner of the temple veranda. He was old and so thin and dried up that he made Muthu think of a snake's transparent skin, no longer needed and left hanging on a thorn. His pale eyes that gazed into eternity flickered briefly to Muthu as the boy put a small coin into his begging bowl. Muthu moved off into the bustle of the bazaar feeling that he had been with the holy man for a very long time, and that they had travelled a long way together.

He was ready to go home, and waiting to get a light for his torch from one of the stalls when he saw Palani arguing with a tailor.

"Ten rupees? Just for some stitching?" Palani was

saying. The tailor's horny feet treddled away on his machine, telling Palani that the tailor did not think Palani was important enough to haggle with.

"Muthu! Muthu, come here!"

Muthu came, slowly, cursing his luck.

"Look at this," Palani said excitedly, pulling at a roll of shimmery pink cloth. "I am having a shirt made from this. What do you think? I shall look like a Bombay film star in this!" Muthu stared at the awful cloth and held back a smile. In such a shirt Palani would be laughed out of the camp.

"Oh yes, Palani," he said encouragingly, "that will make a fine shirt, it will suit you well!"

"You think so? Good. Come, let us go to the tea shop. The newspaper has come." Muthu frowned. He did not trust Palani's sudden, hearty friendship.

"Come," said Palani again. "Wait for me to go back at least, I didn't bring a torch."

Muthu followed his cousin reluctantly. Now he understood. The tea shop was already so crowded that the bamboo walls heaved and bulged. People squatted on the floor, jammed the doorway, perched on the window frames, all chattering and jostling. The tea shop owner climbed on a bench and reached down a tin. He took a pair of steel-rimmed spectacles out of it and hooked them solemnly behind his ears so that he looked very like the photograph of Mahatma Gandhi that hung on the wall and was garlanded on his birthday and on Independence Day.

The crowd were quiet now as he opened the newspaper with a flourish and selected items to read. They only interrupted him to say "What was that? I didn't hear the beginning", or "Who said that, Where was that?" Muthu could not share their fascination. So, someone was murdered in Madras, there were riots far away in Delhi, a strike in Mysore. These things had nothing to do with him and he wanted to go back to the camp.

"Man Crushed by Elephant," read the tea shop owner, and then stopped to clear his throat and enjoy a dramatic pause. His audience—even Muthu—were breathless now with anticipation.

"A forestry worker was found dead near the Amaravathi Dam last Tuesday morning. Dr K. Thomas from the Pollachi hospital, who examined the pitiful remains of the man, believes he was brutally attacked by a rogue elephant. The ground was churned up and the man's tiffin carrier and head cloth were found damaged some distance from the body. There were no witnesses to this gory killing, and there have been no reports of a solitary tusker in the area, but villagers nearby are being told to keep on their guard. . ."

He folded the paper slowly. A buzz of argument had already begun. Trade would be good tonight, he thought happily, as he went to bring in extra charcoal to heat his urn.

"Amaravathi Dam? That is not far, why have we not been warned?"

"It is far. Many miles, near Pollachi."

"That is not far, my brother lives there. And elephants can travel many miles in a night."

"How can they be so sure it was an elephant?"

"What else does it sound like? Elephants can be vicious, you people should know that. Remember when the rogue . . ."

"Elephants are only vicious if they are made so!"

"So they *are* vicious sometimes."

"I didn't say that . . ."

Muthu and Palani and two other boys from the camp gathered round Muthu's torch. The flames made eerie, flickering shadows out of the darkness and they frightened each other with tales of many-headed demons and man-eating panthers. No one mentioned killer rogue elephants. The jungle rustled and creaked and stirred around them. When Muthu strode ahead, the others scrambled to keep up with him and he was pleased. They were afraid of the night jungle, but he, the wild elephant boy who knew nothing, he wasn't afraid.

The next day was a rest day for the elephants and the mahouts gathered round the peepul tree gossiping in the shade. The younger boys who swept the camp and fetched and carried tried to listen to them. The story about the killer elephant had grown in the night and each telling of it had added a freshly invented chapter.

". . . this side of Pollachi, I tell you. Several people gored by its tusks they say . . ."

"It has come from the Anamallais Hills, a giant tusker, ten feet at least . . ."

"*Ten* feet? Aiyh! They have seen it?"

"Many times, it goes onto the roads in full day, like the one we had here."

"That wasn't ten feet tall! But cunning, remember how it lured trackers into the thick jungle, making noises low on the ground like a jungle fowl?"

"And set ambushes on the road through the game reserve, and then attacked the drivers of the vehicles that stopped?"

"It turned over a bus once . . ."

"And the man on the motorbike, remember? It burnt its trunk on the machine and then broke the bike into small bits."

"But who really *knows* about this one? Maybe it is just a bazaar rumour."

"It was in the newspaper last evening."

"Oh! In the *newspaper*!"

There was an uneasy silence. A bad elephant being in the newspaper somehow made it all very real and serious. Muthu had laughed at first to hear grown men, and mahouts at that, gossiping so wildly and topping each other's stories until the real one from the newspaper had disappeared altogether and another had taken its place. He made up his mind that the whole thing had been an accident and there was no bad elephant at all. Elephants were all good to him, and noble, and special to the gods. He found a piece of sugar cane and went to see what the new elephant thought about it all.

The elephant gave him a mean look and shifted his feet grumpily. "You don't mean that," said Muthu confidently, "you're getting to know me now. Come, nice sweet sugar cane. You can take it from my hand today and that will show that we are friends, yes?"

He eased himself between the timbers of the stockade until he was more inside it than outside. He was breathing very slowly and trying to keep his hand steady as he held out the sugar cane. The elephant raised his trunk warily, it wavered, as if he was not sure what to do with it. His eyes moved suspiciously from the sugar cane to Muthu. He must take it. He must, it was so important. Time stopped, there was no sound, there was nothing except this important thing . . .

"Drop the cane. Keep looking at him and climb back very slowly." Rengan's voice was low, slow and totally calm. Muthu did as he was told. He eased himself back through the timbers until Rengan could grasp him and hurl him to the ground. Now he saw his father's face as well, their fear was turning into anger. The elephant trumpeted suddenly and loudly and charged the stockade, making the great structure quiver. Rengan went to calm him, Muthu's father glared at his son.

"You foolish idiot boy! You've got the brain of a slow worm. Don't you know anything about elephants? Going close to a wild one not here a week? You could have been killed, it would have served you right!"

"He was starting to trust me ..." Muthu said truculently. His father pointed to the stockade. "You heard that? *That* is trusting you?"

"But yesterday I talked to him and ... and today ..." His voice was growing shrill, it was just dawning on him that he had been very frightened after all. He ran off towards the jungle. No one was going to listen to his explanations, not in their present mood anyway.

"All his life with elephants!" fumed Muthu's father. "You teach them, you tell them and they do something stupid like that?"

Rengan shrugged. "It was a terrible risk, yes, but ..."

"Yes, all those things. I wouldn't tell Muthu ... but I think this elephant was starting to trust him. Maybe that temper just now, it was because the trust was suddenly broken. That boy has a way with elephants that I have never seen in one so young. I would like to see it in some of the older boys."

"He's mad," said Muthu's father, who had not had time to get over his shock.

"He's all right," Rengan said, "don't worry. He doesn't have many friends, does he?"

"He likes elephants better than people."

Rengan laughed. "So do I most of the time. He talks to them. I have heard him. Tells them what he has been doing, what he thinks, how he feels. They like it, they listen to him. And he gets something back from them, I think."

Muthu's father grunted. "That's why he has no friends. Talking to elephants all the time, they think he's simple in the head!"

3

Muthu went down to the river to have a sulk on his favourite rock, but he found a noisy group of monkeys had taken it over and he decided to stalk them instead. He knew how to move in the jungle: the jungle had been his playground when he was small and had time to play. And Rengan, who had been a tracker as well as a mahout before he became head of the elephant men, had given him much of his knowledge.

  He climbed silently into the tree that hung over the monkeys' rock, upwind of them and hidden by the foliage. He was completely quiet and they were extremely noisy, chattering, fighting and pushing each other about. Gathering some hard green berries, he crawled along the branch like a panther until he was directly above them, and began to ping the berries amongst them. They did not notice at once, but when they did they looked about suspiciously and then blamed each other and started fighting again. A very old and wise monkey, his face wrinkled like a long-forgotten apple, picked up a berry and sniffed it. He smelled Muthu and started jumping up and down waving his arms and giving a strident alarm call. The whole troupe hurled themselves into the tree in one movement. Several of them came across Muthu and started shrieking, baring their vicious little teeth and shaking the branch. Muthu's laughter made them angrier, and he swung out and dropped into the river before they had time to get organised and attack him.

His shirt and dhoti dried in the sun before he got back to the camp. And his resentment had dried up too. The monkeys had taken care of that. Something was happening in the camp, people were running about excitedly and dogs were barking. A stranger was rare in the camp, but this one was spectacular. The camp children stared openly; women left their huts and their fires and came near, putting their saris over their heads to hide their giggles. Only Palani, who swaggered up to him, seemed to recognise the stranger as a fellow human. Muthu could understand that, he was everything Palani dreamed of being. Modern, brash, showy. He wore a violently coloured shirt and European trousers and plastic sandals. His hair was slicked with oil into improbable curves, there was powder on his face and kohl round his eyes and he smelled overpoweringly of sweat and Arabian Nights Pomade.

Everyone was gazing admiringly at his bicycle and some of the young boys were soon ringing the bell and begging rides on it. It was old and rattly with flat tyres, but decorated with tinsel garlands and a bamboo frame with a bright picture of a fat blue-faced god and ladies in glittery clothes that did not seem to fit them properly.

"Muthu! It's the travelling show, they have come to our bazaar!" His elder sisters gathered around him excitedly. "They are doing Krishna stories, with music and dancing . . . and some Ramayana stories and we can go and it will last most of the night!" Muthu glanced towards his mother standing by their hut with a bundle of washing on her head. She smiled and nodded, pleased to see their excitement.

Palani eased himself next to Muthu in the noisy throng. "Rengan will make some of us stay behind," he hissed, "and when he asks who will stay, it will be you." Muthu walked away. He wouldn't mind staying. But he did mind Palani telling him he had to.

The travelling show was one part of the excitement. But because it was so unexpected and rare, getting ready for it was an event in itself. Even Muthu found his best shirt and dhoti that he wore sometimes for weddings and festivals. He teased his sisters as they spent hours plaiting flowers into each other's hair. And then, suddenly, the laughing, joyful crowd had gone and it was quiet again.

Muthu, of course, had not gone. But neither had Palani or Rengan. It was quite fair—to everyone except Palani—as the show went on so long a rota was drawn up amongst the youngsters, so that two of them would always be in the camp in case Rengan needed them. There was nothing for them to do once they had brought the water and tidied the camp. The working elephants were all loose in the jungle, there were no sick or injured needing attention. Palani wandered about moodily. Muthu squatted with Rengan, watching his leathery hands carving toys for his grandchildren. It was strange being with Rengan and not working. He was in a silent mood and Muthu knew better than to interrupt him.

He had once made the bad mistake of asking Rengan why he never rode an elephant, not even when he had to go out to the logging site. Rengan had given him such a ferocious glare that he had not dared to speak to him again for a week. He wished that Rengan would talk to him about his elephant because the mystery intrigued him. The other mahouts would not talk about it either, except to say it had been a temperamental one-tusked beast. They had not liked it and Muthu knew there had to be a reason. He had not been around when it died, but he knew that Rengan had buried its one tusk deep in the jungle where no ivory dealer or poacher would ever find it. And he knew that Rengan still treasured the first tip that had been sawn off the tusk when it started working. Now he would not even ride old Meenakshi. Old one-tusk had been as special as that.

Rengan sighed and looked wistfully out across the jungle as if he was remembering his elephant. Suddenly Muthu realised he was not.

"You are thinking about that big fish you told me about?" Muthu said, as respectfully as he could. Rengan nodded and smiled distantly. His fishing was a gentle joke in the camp. He often went off in the evening with his spear and a net and rarely caught anything. But he didn't mind that, it was the fishing he enjoyed and so did his old pi-dog. The river glinted temptingly in the sun. Why not? Rengan reasoned. He had thought of sending the boys off because there was nothing to do, but this was a much better idea. Palani thought so too.

"Yes, Rengan, you go fishing. We will be all right here."

"You promise not to go near the new one, Muthu? He has all he needs."

"Yes. Shall I light a fire to cook the fish?" Rengan cuffed him lightly and was gone. Before he had even reached the river, Palani had beetled off too. It was very quiet, there were only old people left in the camp and some mothers with their smallest children. Muthu walked round proudly, hoping that someone would say Hey! Who is in charge of the camp? And then he could say *I am*! There is no one else here! He went over to tell the new elephant how important he felt. He squatted a little distance from the stockade and chuntered on gently to the elephant until he swayed, mesmerised by Muthu's voice and Muthu nearly dozed off himself.

Suddenly he was alert: there was a movement in the jungle across the camp, a grey shape loomed out of the jungle. "Meenakshi!" said Muthu happily. "What are you doing here? Why . . . Meenakshi?" He rushed to meet her. It was obvious why she had come back: she was sick, very sick and she had come for help. She lumbered in slowly and painfully and stopped, resting her trunk against the rail round the cookhouse where the elephants lined up for their food and medicines.

Muthu panicked. He rushed to Rengan's tin trunk where the drugs were kept and wrestled with the padlock and hammered on the lid. He rushed back to Meenakshi. Her eyes looked cloudy with pain, she was shifting her feet as if the weight of her stomach was too great to carry. Stomach pains, Muthu thought, indigestion, elephants got a lot of that, especially old ones. She lifted one of her feet, and then bent her leg hesitantly.

"No, Meenakshi," Muthu screamed in horror, "don't lie down, you mustn't lie down!" She looked at him blearily and her great head waved from side to side as if she was trying to tell him that she wouldn't do a silly thing like that, but then a new wave of pain came and she lifted one foot again tentatively. Chinoo! Muthu felt a tremor of relief. Chinoo was in the camp, his father's kavadi! He rushed to his hut. Chinoo's wife stopped him at the door.

"Muthu, what is it? Chinoo is sick, you can't go in."

"He must come. Meenakshi is very sick, she may

lie down. Chinoo must come, he must get Lakshmi to hold her up." Muthu pleaded with wild eyes and Chinoo's wife shook him roughly by the shoulders. She had been raised amongst elephants, her father was a mahout at Theppakkadu, she glanced at Meenakshi and understood. "Chinoo cannot walk," she said. "I will come." They ran together to Meenakshi, who swayed uncomfortably.

"Muthu! Come away," Chinoo's wife shrieked. "She will fall on you." Muthu ran and beat his hands against Meenakshi's sides in a frenzy of frustration. Chinoo's wife dragged a leafy branch from the edge of the camp.

"Use this," she gasped. "I will run to the bazaar for mahouts. But be careful!"

C. P. Vishnuswamy, Assistant Veterinary Surgeon based at Theppakkadu, known simply, but respectfully, as Vishnu-Vet, was driving past the turn-off to the smaller camp that afternoon. His jeep bumped and rattled through the jungle, he was hot and tired. Suddenly the thought of a couple of hours' fishing with Rengan seemed a very good idea. He could spare the time and he knew Rengan would be glad of the excuse to take him, so why not? The camp was curiously quiet for the time of day, even though it was a rest day. There was just one elephant, old Meenakshi he judged from a distance, a cluster of children round her. They heard the jeep and several of them came running to meet him, waving their arms and shouting wildly.

The jeep shuddered to a stop. Vishnu grabbed his bag and only then did he see Muthu and realise the horror of the situation. Muthu was almost underneath Meenakshi, lashing at her with a frayed branch and shouting, "Don't go down! Stay up, you fool, stay up!" The elephant swayed dangerously, her knee went down on the ground, and Vishnu hurled himself at Muthu and threw him out of danger. Meenakshi turned her head to see what was happening, her leg straightened again, her eyes fastened beseechingly on Vishnu.

"How long?" snapped Vishnu, opening his bag and filling a syringe.

"Half an hour..." Muthu gasped. "She was going to..."

"Where's Rengan? Mahouts. Get two elephants brought in..." He stopped suddenly, glanced around. "Where *is* everyone?" he demanded furiously, and rammed the big needle into Meenakshi's tough hide. He sighed and wiped the sweat out of his eyes. "Keep on your feet old lady," he breathed, like a prayer. And then he swore at every mahout that ever lived, and particularly the ones in this camp that left a child in charge of a dying elephant!

It was two hours before Vishnu was confident that Meenakshi was out of danger. He had moved the jeep next to her and sat in it writing his report for her record book. Muthu was perched on the rail, reaching uncomfortably to massage Meenakshi's great forehead, his arms aching, his palms sore.

"You don't have to do that now," Vishnu said, grinning up at him.

"I know I don't," said Muthu, "but I do really. She has no mahout."

Vishnu grunted. It was almost funny, now that the drama was over, a slight boy holding up five tons of elephant. He might have saved her life. But he would not put that in the report, the elephant men had lost too much face as it was. They had come rushing back, summoned by Chinoo's wife when the crisis was over. Rengan had come back triumphantly with a fine mahseer. It had lain where he had dropped it, fly blown and drying in the sun, until the dogs had eaten it. Rengan should not have been so upset, Muthu thought, how could he have known what was going to happen? Palani had been caught by the rage of his guilt when he tried to slink back unnoticed. That had been worth seeing!

But it had been close for Meenakshi. She had so nearly gone, she had looked at them, begging them to let her go. Several times she had quivered and once she had even knelt. But they had gone on, shouting, thrashing at her with leafy boughs and she had believed them and stayed up until the injection worked. Muthu wished he had done more for her, done something important. Twice Vishnu had shouted at him to get out of the way and he had cringed. He had wanted to be a hero for Vishnu. Vishnu had been his hero for a long time now, but he had been angry when Muthu ran off.

"Where are you going?"
"To get my father's elephant. She will help."
"No. Come back, I will not allow it!"
"I can do it. She is not far."
"Come back. Do as you're told."

It hadn't been very heroic. "I could have brought my father's elephant in," he said now, trying to improve on what had happened, "she would have come for me."

"Yes?" said Vishnu vaguely.

"My father's kavadi is ill with fever. Tomorrow I will go with my father to bring Lakshmi in, and one day . . . it will be my elephant I bring in." He peered down to see what Vishnu was thinking. He did not seem to be taking much notice. "I will have my own elephant . . . be kavadi, then mahout." Vishnu stopped writing, but he did not look at Muthu.

"Will you still be vet here when I have my elephant?"

Vishnu went on writing for a little while. "Vet here? I will always come here sometimes, though not always all the time."

"You can't stop looking after the elephants! Since you have been coming, none of them have died!"

"No," said Vishnu, thinking with satisfaction that although he had nearly lost one just two hours ago, it was true. He had been lucky; there had been no serious accidents. No rabies, or foot-and-mouth disease, smallpox or Black Quarter. Being young he had modern ideas. He spent long and tedious days inoculating cattle in the villages all around the camps so that the cattle could not spread their diseases.

"The old vet, not the last one, he didn't stay, the one before that, he didn't always give anthrax injections."

"He didn't?" said Vishnu, amused that a camp child should speak to him so openly. They were usually shy and withdrawn with him. He could learn a lot from Muthu, he thought, that would be useful to him. Things perhaps that the elephant men wouldn't tell him.

"No, he didn't," said Muthu, feeling encouraged. "Not when he was afraid of an elephant. And the mahouts did all the worm treatment, and they tipped the elephants' tusks themselves, down in the river. They said he cut them too high. If you had been here when Rengan's elephant . . ."

"Rengan's elephant? He never speaks of it. Did he die of anthrax?"

"I don't know," Muthu said quickly, he was on dangerous ground. "Why did you say you would come sometimes but not all times?"

Vishnu thought how he could explain this to Muthu. "You know how a kavadi trains an elephant from when it is small?"

"Yes," said Muthu mystified.

"And then the elephant grows and starts work, and the kavadi becomes mahout. But he goes on training him even when he is fully grown. Well, it is the same with me. I have been trained by kavadis at my college, but soon I will go and be trained some more by mahouts in Bombay, even though I am grown up too."

Muthu stared at him comically. "You, Vishnu-Vet? Go to school? But you write things down and drive a jeep already!"

"There is much to learn about elephants, it's called research . . . you go on searching for more and more knowledge. I shall take what I have learned here and use that to learn more, do you see?"

"Yes," said Muthu thoughtfully. "So you will be made mahout from kavadi and then you will earn four hundred and fifty rupees a month and not just four hundred and forty-five. But . . . Bombay is very far, isn't it?"

"I will go there in an aeroplane. And maybe if I work hard I will come back as a State Vet, in charge of all the working elephants in South India."

Muthu frowned. He did not like to look ahead to a time when Vishnu would not be there.

"Will you stay all night with Meenakshi?" he said instead.

"No. She will be all right. Rengan will see to her. I'll give her another injection soon."

"What is wrong with her?"

"She is old, seventy. Her last teeth are wearing down and she can't eat the right sort of food any more so her stomach suffers. I have written in her book that she should have more fodder brought in for her, and I've given her extra rations. In the jungle she would have died of starvation by now, that is the way with wild ones."

"I don't like it when elephants lie down," said Muthu suddenly. Vishnu looked at him curiously. "Why do you say that?"

Muthu stared out into the darkness. "I saw Lakshmi lie down, here in the camp one night and I was frightened. Elephants are very big sideways. Maybe that is what I don't like. The bigness."

"They are too heavy to lie down for very long. I know what you mean. I have watched elephants at night and it is eerie. They choose a particular time and they stop eating and stand very still. They listen, and the jungle listens with them, and piece by piece it becomes silent. But really silent, there is not an insect moving, the wind is still. And then it is time and they lie down slowly and you think the whole world has stopped and you wait, hardly breathing... and then they are up again and eating, eating, eating!"

"If Meenakshi had lain down today?"

"She would have died. Her intestines are weakened, her weight would have crushed them. Even with two tuskers to lift her, I don't think we would have got her back on her feet."

"Rengan told me that long ago they used to light a fire under a sick elephant to keep it up."

"I know. I thought of that today. If she had got worse, if we could not find two elephants to hold her up in time . . . No, I would not have used fire. To do that, you are crossing a wild threshold that you should not cross."

"I don't know what you mean," said Muthu.

"You will find out."

Palani caught up with Muthu later that evening and threw him into a lantana bush with a force that took his breath away. Muthu saw the grass-cutting knife glint in the moonlight. "No, Palani," he gasped, clutching his throat. Palani's voice cracked with rage. "*You* got me into trouble, you again!"

"You went away when you were told to stay, that's my fault?"

"Everyone is angry, not just Rengan. And you! Winding like a skinny snake, Muthu here, Muthu there, being so courageous and useful. Creeping, crawling to get me into trouble. Muthu sitting there talking to Vishnu-Vet as if he was just anyone! Everyone saw you, you wanted them to see you with him. You wanted to show me up."

"You show yourself up, I don't need to do that. Anyone can see that you don't care about elephants, you're not interested."

Palani drew back and threw his knife aside. He didn't need it now. He had something that would hurt Muthu more than any knife could.

"I will have an elephant soon," he said unpleasantly, "and then you, you grass-cutter, dung-clearer, you will work for me. You will work hard."

"You don't want an elephant," said Muthu angrily. "You want a city job. So why don't you go there and find one?"

"Because I can't, can I? I have to be mahout, there is nothing else."

"I will get an elephant soon after you."

"No," said Palani triumphantly, "I have heard Government news from Madras, I heard from my friend at Theppakkadu."

"What?"

"After me there will be no more new mahouts in this camp for many years. And by then you will be too old to have an elephant. Government have said this camp is not to get bigger. I will be the last mahout."

"I don't believe it!" Muthu said with a sickening dread building in his stomach that meant he probably did.

"Ask your father. Ask Rengan. Ask your grand friend Vishnu-Vet."

"They would have told me."

"They only just heard. They don't like to tell you in case you squeal like a monkey and stamp your feet!"

"I will go to Theppakkadu, then."

"You don't belong there. And they have enough kavadis waiting. Believe me, Muthu, it is true. There will be an elephant for me, but there will never be one for you!"

4

There could be no sleeping that night. Muthu thrashed about on his string cot trying to get away from the unbearable thing Palani had said. *An elephant for me . . . never an elephant for you, never, never . . .* When Palani got his elephant Muthu would have to run away. Where could he go? What did he know? He couldn't go to a place where there were no elephants. *Ask Rengan, ask your father . . .* He couldn't do that, not yet. They would tell him the truth and he wasn't ready for it. Maybe Palani was lying. Maybe his lie would go away. No. It was there. *Ask your grand friend Vishnu-Vet . . .* But he had asked Vishnu-Vet just today. Not a question exactly, but when he had talked about being a mahout, Vishnu had stopped writing but he had not looked at him. He had not said—yes, Muthu, soon—or—you will be a good mahout, Muthu. He had not said anything at all. He had stopped writing but he had refused to look at Muthu.

Normally the jungle sounds lulled him to sleep. Tonight they were harsh and mocking and kept him awake. A sambhur stag sounded his haunting bell-call near the camp, but this time Muthu did not care whether it was answered or whether the sambhur stayed out there all alone. A herd of red-spotted chital crossed the river: a big herd, their splashing went on for several minutes. Muthu did not picture them in his mind that night, see them splashing, wading, swimming, wading again and scrambling up the bank on the far side, their hundreds of alert, pretty heads above the water; a proud stag, his antlers spread like a tree, waiting, counting on the far bank; anxious mothers nudging and pushing their fawns. They didn't matter, they could drown. A wild tusker trumpeted in the distance, checking the area. A camp elephant grazing close to the camp responded. So did Meenakshi. Muthu heard them stirring, the faint rattle of their chains. It was no comfort to know they were so close that night. So close he could hear them rumbling, munching, hear the thud of their droppings on the hard earth. He was glad when the dawn pushed its way through the gaps in the thatch and he no longer had to try and trap sleep to escape his worst fears. Today he was going with his father to bring Lakshmi in. When they were alone together in the jungle, *then* he would find out the truth.

The night mist still hugged the ground near the river and as they went through the tall grass Muthu got drenched up to his shoulders with dew. They startled some deer drinking at the river, who gave shrill warning cries to each other and were gone in an elegant kicking of hooves. They took a detour round a bison family, standing neatly in their white socks. Coming back on Lakshmi they would be part of the jungle and could pass any creatures unnoticed, but now they were not part of its wildness and must respect its defences.

Muthu plunged ahead, hoping to impress his father with his tracking skill. He followed the marks of Lakshmi's feet and her drag chain and noted professionally where she had stopped and what she had been eating. Some elephants came to meet their kavadis when they called and some just went on eating or even hid until the last moment. Each one had its own habits and sense of humour. Two miles out, Muthu kicked over a pile of dung and examined it.

"And what does that tell you?" his father asked.

"She was here two . . . three hours ago? She has had enough bamboo, so . . . she has gone this way, where it is wetter for grass . . . or that way where the jungle is thicker for roots."

"Yes, but which way?"

"I don't know, and I can't find the trail in this thorny stuff." His father laughed and climbed on to a rock and called to Lakshmi. Then he settled down to wait.

Ask him now Muthu, now!

"This time she has gone all the way to Mysore," he said instead, pushing the question away.

"Lakshmi? Never would she go more than four miles."

"But you didn't teach her that."

"The drag chain tells her that. Her bell reminds her."

"She could take the chain to Mysore. It is nothing, just a chain. What would she do if you didn't put the chain on?"

"She wouldn't understand what was happening then. I know how she thinks."

"You like bringing her in, don't you? Why don't you do it all the time?"

"Because that is kavadi's job, isn't it. Why are you always supposing things that don't happen, Muthu?"

Now. Ask him now!

"Rajiv will come soon, he is to have the new elephant. How long will he take to tame?"

"He is young, maybe two weeks and he will forget he was ever wild. Even the grown elephants we used to catch, they only took about forty days." He was quiet, thinking about them. Remembering the last khedda years ago, when a herd of forty wild elephant had been rounded up and driven into a vast stockade. It had taken months of preparation, vast crowds had come to watch the final stages. Muthu loved to hear the story, how he and Lakshmi had been chosen to go in among the wild elephants and rope them . . . It had been dangerous, exciting . . . it had saddened him too, seeing the panic-stricken elephants.

"Will there be other wild elephants coming, like that one?" said Muthu.

"No. It is not allowed. Elephants are protected, you can't just take them from the wild any more. That is why we breed them in the camps."

"There are several calves coming," said Muthu slowly, "but . . . but Palani says . . ." His father got up and called to Lakshmi again. Muthu picked at some moss on the rock and disturbed an ants' nest. The ants ran over his hand, but he didn't notice.

"Palani says I will never have my own elephant."

"Palani says that?"

"Is it true? It isn't true! Government says we have enough in our camp and after Palani . . . after Palani . . ." His voice was rising squeakily like a young animal crying out.

"I don't know these things."

"You do know! You must know. You are mahout. But me? I won't even be kavadi."

"Muthu, you are good with elephants. There will always be work for you with elephants."

"I can be grass cutter?" said Muthu savagely, "be sweeper, water carrier, log boy, rope mender . . . never mahout."

"There will be a kavadi job sometime."

"Not kavadi going on to mahout. Just kavadi to someone else's elephant. Not *my* elephant."

Muthu's father sighed deeply. He had known that this moment would come. His wife had said—Why don't you tell the boy? Tell him, I say! Don't let him go on thinking, hoping . . . What if it had been *you*?

"Chinoo will never be a mahout," he said, "he is too old now. But he is happy taking care of Lakshmi for me. Rengan! You could be like Rengan, help with doctoring the elephants."

"Rengan was mahout first. But more elephants will be born in our camp, Government can't stop that, can they?"

"They will go to Theppakkadu. Our camp is not to get bigger. The head forest man from Madras said so himself. They make good tractors in Bangalore now. Machines for lifting, pulling . . ."

"Machines can't do what Lakshmi can do," said Muthu, drawing on one of his father's favourite arguments. "Can a machine think so well it can balance a one ton log on a pile *exactly*? Does it remember all about the jungle when it goes in, so it knows the best way to come out pulling a log? Does it listen to you, pick up things? Does it . . ."

"Stop, Muthu! These are things *I* have told you! Things elephant people have known since the foreign people first brought their machines into our jungles. I am not Government, *I* do not say you cannot have an elephant." He jumped down from the rock and reached up to lift Muthu down as if he was still a small child, and staggered back with him.

"You're so heavy! I remember when I used to carry you for miles but now . . ."

"Now I am big enough to be mahout."

His father spun on him like an angry tiger. "I know!" he shouted. "Don't tell me, Muthu, I know!"

Lakshmi knew she had to leave the juicy grass she had found. She pulled up one last clump, slapped the roots lazily on her raised foot to dislodge the earth and stuffed it into her mouth as she ambled slowly towards her mahout.

"I could bring Lakshmi in myself, couldn't I?" Muthu asked as they swayed towards the camp.

"She would come for you, I expect, but . . ."

"Can I do it tomorrow?"

His father hesitated. He wanted to say no, knew he should say no. But how could he when he had just shattered his son's dreams?

"Tomorrow then. But just this one time, you understand."

The horror, the tragedy, and yes, the drama and excitement too, built up slowly during the day, scene after scene, like the travelling show. The news came in bits and pieces from the bazaar to the camp, where the story was fitted together.

"Did you hear? Sita the baker's wife is missing! She went to collect firewood early this morning!"

"She will come back."

"It has been hours now . . ."

"Maybe she met someone. She does, you know."

"All the same, they are sending people to look for her."

"She is still not found! I wouldn't blame her if she had gone running. What a life she has with that fellow!"

"Where would she go? She has relatives close?"

"They have found Sita. She is dead!"

"He murdered her? What did I tell you about him!"

"No, no! Not like that. She was crushed against a rock. Completely crushed and all her firewood thrown here and there as though some mad thing . . . there were no screams. Nothing. *It was a silent killing.*"

The camp was silent too, muffled by a cloud of doom and dread. Dread that the silent killing meant an elephant killing. The Range Officer came to see Rengan. He was aggressive at first. Of course he could account for the movements of all the camp elephants, most of them were at work, weren't they? No, none were on musth, if they were they would be secured, wouldn't they? Grudgingly he admitted he was an experienced tracker and, yes, he knew a bit about elephants. He would come.

A lot of the camp people went too, drifting off towards the bazaar trying to conceal their fascination and horror about what had happened. But if an elephant was involved, in some way it concerned them all. Muthu thought so too.

A crowd had pressed around the rock where the woman had been killed, a noisy, jostling, curious crowd and Muthu thought they were wrong and should be quiet. Some women threw their saris over their heads and started wailing, and some were sick. Two policemen and a forester were trying to keep people away from the rock. Muthu, being small and slight, filtered through them and was suddenly and sickeningly confronted with the death place. He had scarcely known Sita, and there was nothing to see of her now. They had taken away what might have remained, there were just some scraps of blood-stained sari and broken glass from her bangles. Muthu was used to death. It was always around in the jungle—creature killed creature as a way of living. But this was something else and it had no reason behind it. He had seen dead people too, death was a public thing and he had followed funeral processions and seen bodies burned like everyone else. But you knew why the people had died and you did not have to think how.

Rengan squatted in the dust shrugging hopelessly. "You should have kept the people away. They have trampled everywhere." There had been an elephant in the area and he was puzzled by it. He asked for a piece of string to measure round a footmark it had left. "Less than four feet," he said, holding it up, "so this elephant would be less than eight feet at the shoulder, quite small."

The police inspector turned to the forester. "That is some jungle tale, isn't it? You can't tell the height from the foot."

"Sixty years I have worked with elephants,"

Rengan said angrily, "twice round the foot is always the height. Exactly. It has never been wrong."

"All right, old man, what else?"

Rengan glared at the men. "It is hard to say, *now*! The droppings show it is a sick elephant, maybe an old one who can't eat properly . . . you have walked over the other marks, there was one smaller . . . she could have an injured foot . . . from a snare perhaps?"

"Why do you keep saying 'she'? It must have been a tusker, a rogue. They do things like this, not females." Rengan stood up ignoring them and stared across the scrubby brown jungle to the beginning of a shallow valley. He could not tell where she had gone, she was cunning.

"People must be warned," the police inspector said. "Write down 'injured rogue male elephant, extremely dangerous'."

"I said a female, small, underweight and sick," said Rengan grittily. "I am not sure that she is very old, she may be quite young. But something bad has happened to her."

"Guesswork," muttered the inspector, but Rengan heard.

"Why did you bring me here if you don't listen to what I say? Is this how you protect people? Tell them to look out for the wrong animal? If someone else dies it will be your fault!" Muthu followed at a safe distance as Rengan strode off, steaming with anger.

He did not dare to speak until Rengan's pace slowed, his head lowered from fury to dejection.

"Rengan?"

"Go away, Muthu. Leave me alone!"

He followed Rengan quietly for a mile and then they came to a leafy clearing. A trickle of water oozed down the rock face and made a small pool. Rengan drank from it and washed his face. "Come out from behind that tree, Muthu," he said tiredly, "I am not angry with you."

"Why would she do such a thing?" Muthu asked, showing his concern, showing he believed what Rengan had said.

"Why? Why?" He sighed deeply. "She had a reason. She must have had a good reason to do that," he gestured over his shoulder. "You should not have seen it."

"Rengan, you have known a she-elephant be bad before?"

"Yes. It doesn't happen often. But when it does . . . it is a very terrible thing. Worse than a male, many times worse. It's worse than those fools back there know."

"What will happen now?"

"Nothing. Oh, they will talk and write reports about the wrong elephant and get all important about it. But nothing will happen. Not until she kills someone else. Or they find it is the same elephant that killed the man near Pollachi. That is possible."

"And then . . . ?"

"No one is allowed to shoot an elephant until it is proscribed—that means it has to be proved to be very dangerous, a definite killer. Then there is a licence to shoot it and everyone for hundreds of miles will come who has a gun and wants to be a hero. Harmless tuskers will probably get shot, yes, and their tusks will mysteriously disappear. Last time it happened here an innocent elephant was shot and the bad one died of tetanus twenty miles away!"

The elephants felt the camp's uneasiness as soon as they came back from work, it was very strong. Even kavadis, who did not like to admit fear, went about in twos or threes. Small children needed no warning, they would not even go to the lavatory hut alone.

Muthu's dilemma was different. His father had promised him that he could fetch Lakshmi alone the next day. He had not said, "Don't go now Muthu, after what has happened." He would not expect him to do anything so stupid. But he had to do something so stupid, it was very important to him. A real elephant man would face any danger for his elephant; he could do that too. He did not want to be a hero. Just a mahout.

He left the camp before it was light and anyone was around to stop him. He soon wished that someone *would* stop him, he was more alone and frightened in the darkness than he had ever been in his life. The jungle throbbed with hunters, hunting, hunted, he felt threatened by its breathing, rustling, snorting. The distant dong of an elephant bell was reassuring, big old Raja was not far away. Muthu wanted to rush to him and cower between his front legs, seeking protection like a young calf.

He reached the clearing where Lakshmi always came in the early evening. Now he would have to wait until the sky lightened some more before he could pick up her trail. He sat cautiously on a fallen tree and watched the dawn glowing through every shade of pink and orange. Shapes came into focus and the dawn wind stirred the bamboo and made it click. A porcupine had met its gory death in the clearing during the night, its bent and bloodied quills were scattered on the jungle floor. Muthu had kept an orphaned porcupine once in an enclosure he made out of woven branches and leaves. He liked the way it put up its quills like an umbrella when it was frightened, and charged backwards stamping its little human feet. He was going to free it in the jungle when it was big enough, but the men ate it and told him how good it tasted. Better than wild pig, or chicken, sweet and tender. He had tried to laugh with them to show he was grown up. But he had smelt it cooking and remembered the little stamping feet.

Lakshmi's trail was easy to follow, he was getting close to her when it occurred to him that she would not be pleased to see him so early and would probably refuse to come until the proper time. He slowed down. Another elephant trail crossed Lakshmi's and he started to follow it curiously because it was odd. There were unhealthy droppings, he would find out who it was and tell Rengan. It had strange eating habits too. Where he would have expected to find tall bamboo pulled down, it was still standing, there was none of the blaze of destruction that most elephants left behind them. Small bushes had been stripped, a lot of bulbs and roots kicked out of the ground. Then he realised something he should have noticed first of all. There was no drag chain.

He followed the trail until it left the heavy jungle and went across open scrub land. No place for an elephant, but this one had gone on. He shaded his eyes, the scrub continued, broken up by rocks until it plunged down towards the river. There was a patch of bare earth at the edge of the jungle. Muthu stared at it, a buzz of fear and excitement mingled in his head. He crouched on the ground, the footmarks were clear, there were two sets. One belonged to an adult elephant, not very big, not as heavy as Lakshmi. He remembered the droppings and Rengan's words the day before. "You're right, Rengan, it is a sick female elephant. But you were wrong about the deformed foot. She has a young calf!"

There was just time, before the kavadis came, if he ran all the way he could cross the scrub jungle and climb onto the distant rock. And from there he would be able to see for miles in every direction.

There was nothing to be seen. He climbed down the far side of the rock, there was a gully leading steeply down to the river. He scrambled to the edge of the cliff and then let himself down onto a ledge from where he could look down to the river. There was a sandy bay at the bottom of the rugged cliff.

She was there, below, merging greyly into the background. She gave a little squeal of warning and the baby came to her, puzzled. A male, thin, Muthu thought, about a year old, maybe more. The mother turned slightly. And then Muthu saw her trunk.

5

Muthu turned away with tears stinging his eyes and a knot in his throat. A third of her trunk was a mass of hideous sores, raw and weeping. The whole trunk was swollen into a tortured shape. He steeled himself to look again. She reached out her trunk to her baby and gave a squeal of pain. She was eyeing him now with terrible hatred and suspicion. "No," Muthu said chokily, "don't hate me. I didn't do it. I want to help you. Stay here where you're safe and I'll . . . I'll . . ." He didn't know what he was going to do, only that it had to be soon and it had to be miraculous. And it had to be secret.

Lakshmi was so surprised to see Muthu on his own that she came to him at once and knelt for him. As he reached up, grasping a handful of spare skin as a handhold, she put her trunk protectively round his back. She had never done that before. He was touched because she realised he was small and unprotected. He did not think that it was also because she could feel his sense of outrage and sadness about the terrible thing he had seen.

Muthu mastered his tears and his shaking. He must forget for the moment that pitiful sight or it would show in his face. He felt fiercely proud high up on Lakshmi, bringing her in alone. He could hear kavadis shouting to their elephants, and did not note the panic in their voices. Wait till they saw *him*!

It was not a moment of triumph at all. His father and two other mahouts suddenly burst through the jungle following Lakshmi's trail. They did not greet him, they turned and their practised calls echoed back through the jungle—"Muthu is safe!—All's well, Muthu is found!" And then they turned on him. Was he mad, going off alone? Even mahouts didn't do that. His mother was out of her head with worry. The whole camp was searching, he was a disgrace to his family, he'd upset the whole camp routine . . .

His mother started when he got back. "Muthu, there is a killer elephant out there! It will kill again, maybe many times and maybe one of those times it will be you!"

"I *have* to get out of the camp," Muthu said desperately. The new elephant gave a little snort. "Oh, you can snort. You don't have my problems, do you?" He squatted a little closer to the stockade. Rengan glanced over occasionally, checking on him. He was scouring out the big cooking dekshis with sand and a twist of rope. "Listen, you are fit and cared for and Rajiv will come soon, but this one I have seen . . . you would not *believe*, it is so awful. I can't tell anyone but you, it is the one that killed Sita yesterday. Rengan was right, it is a she and she has a good reason to hate people. I know why she does . . . and this is hard to tell you . . . it is hard just to know it . . ." He stopped and swallowed hard. "She has been shot in her trunk, it is badly infected . . . I know what happened because I have seen pictures. Visiting Vet and the Range Officer came and we all had to sit round and be told about poachers and traps and things. They showed us pictures, there was one of an elephant that had been shot with one of those blunder-things that villagers use to scare wild animals off their crops. And this one, she looks just the same, so I know. The Range Officer told us to report . . . if we ever came across poaching or . . . or saw an injured animal . . . well, I have found one and I can't tell *anyone*!" He stopped, sniffed and attacked the dekshis with fury. "You understand, don't you? If I tell anyone, she will be shot. But it wasn't her fault she killed the baker's wife. It was the fault of whoever shot her and made her hate people so much. So, I have to take her medicines and food to make her better. And when she is better, maybe she will trust me, and know that not all people are bad. She has a baby, she must take it back to her herd."

It was not difficult for Muthu to steal because Rengan trusted him and left him alone when the food and medicine chests were unlocked. He took vitamins that he knew were good for weak elephants, pills that Rengan gave them for fevers and infections and mixed them up with generous helpings of horsegram and jaggery, rice and coconut and salt. He stole a little at a time, tucking handfuls into a fold in his dhoti and transferring them to a hollow tree behind his hut. When he had as much as he could manage he found a piece of hessian that smelled strongly of elephant, and made a bundle that he hoped would not smell of himself at all.

Getting away was the difficult part. In desperation he told his mother and Rengan and Palani different things that he was going to be doing, and made his secret way out of the camp. He ran all the way. She had chosen her hiding place well, no one would ever look for her there. It was mere chance that he had found her.

She had turned round to face out of the sun. The baby was playing in the river, solemnly, Muthu thought. He didn't have the usual baby-elephant jollity. He supposed they went out at night to get their fodder. Except for yesterday. What had she been doing near the bazaar in day time? Would she go out again in the day? He prayed that she would not, it was obvious she could not use her trunk to pull down food, she must raid crops that were easy for her to root up, easy for the baby. She must get well soon, it was too dangerous for her to go near villages. He tipped his bundle over the cliff and it scattered over the rock beside her. She stirred suspiciously, the baby looked curious—but would she eat it? Would she let the baby eat it? It had been as much as he could carry but now it seemed pathetically little. What was he doing? For the first time he had a niggling doubt. Was he just extending her agony, could he really do anything for her? Should he let her die in peace? But then there was the baby. The argument raged inside him and it was as if there were two people in him pushing and pulling at his guts, at his heart. He turned to go feeling miserable.

He climbed back a different way, a steeper, more difficult way but it would be quicker. Half-way up he came to a ledge covered in creeper, and the creeper gave against his weight. He started to pull it away, watching out for scorpions or snakes. There was a space in the rocks like an open cave. Muthu stopped to rest, thinking it would be a good place to hide, or to store things. It smelt very old, slightly mysterious. He explored it half afraid, and then he realised that it was an ancient shrine, forgotten perhaps for centuries. There was an image at the far end, crude and worn, but the sight of it filled Muthu with pure joy. It was *him*! With his pot belly and his fat thighs, the human, in-turned feet, the elephant head with its wise eyes and stumpy little tusks, the extra hands holding the lotus and the staff ... Ganesha, the elephant-headed god. The god of wisdom whom you worshipped when you started a hard task! The god who took difficulties out of the way, showed you the way ahead. Ganesha! Here!

Muthu pulled back in awe. "Ganesha! So it was meant to be," he whispered. "I was meant to come and find these elephants. You brought me here!" He shook his head and grinned with delight. It was meant to be! He had stolen and he had told lies for the elephants. But that was all right now, it was meant to be, he need not feel guilty any more. The elephant would get better and go back to her herd. Everything was suddenly fitting into place. There were a few grains of rice stuck to the hessian. Muthu scraped them off, and he pulled some wild orchid flowers off the rock and gave them to the little god. "It is all I have this time," he said earnestly, "but I will be back tomorrow."

As the days slipped by the drama of Sita's death faded. There was no evidence of a rogue elephant in the area and the elephant men began to wonder if it had been an accident after all. An elephant on musth could have done it. Trained elephants had killed their own mahouts before when the madness of musth was on them. It was something elephant people could understand and forgive. Perhaps it wasn't an elephant at all, but a bison, master bulls could be dangerous, couldn't they? People started to move about more freely and it was easier for Muthu to escape. He had given the elephants names now, Ama for the mother and Tumbu for the baby. The food and medicines he dropped were always gone the next day but he couldn't be sure who had eaten them. Sometimes he thought Ama was looking better and Muthu felt a thrill of pride. And then she was worse. Horribly worse. Muthu stared at her and then he wept as he had never done before. She was standing in the river looking gaunt and hopeless. The swelling on her trunk was grotesque, she was trying to fill it with water and squirt it over her back, but each time she tried to raise it she gave a squeal-grunt of pain. She was feverish now, Muthu could tell that. She did not even care that he was there. He emptied the bundle onto the rocks below and went to the shrine to put the coconut and hibiscus flowers he had brought in front of Ganesha.

"She isn't getting any better," he said sullenly. "What is the matter? Don't I bring you enough? Don't I pray all the time? Well? What do I do now? Tell me. Do you want her to die? Do you think she is wicked? Ganesha, you can't let her go on suffering this way, help me. Give me a sign." He waited, wondering what a sign from the gods would be like and if he'd recognise it when it came. Nothing happened at all.

"That's your answer then, silence. Then I shall have to look after her my way. I shall do it tomorrow, you'll see!"

Muthu was so worried about Ama that he became reckless, not just with the things he stole but the things he said as well.

"When does Vishnu-Vet come again?" he asked Rengan innocently.

"Tomorrow, I hope. There is hardly enough ointment left for Raja's sore. What do you boys do, eat it?"

"Did I put on too much yesterday?" he asked meekly, and Rengan grunted. "It's powerful, isn't it, like magic? If Raja's sore was poisoned, would you put the same ointment on?"

"I don't let sores get poisoned, do I?"

"No, but if?"

"Yes, yes," said Rengan impatiently, "it cures anything. If we had such ointment years ago ... well, we wouldn't have lost Jaya after his fight. Ah, that was an elephant you should have known, Muthu!"

"He fought a wild tusker, didn't he?" asked Muthu cautiously. "What do you think happened to *that* one? With no one to look after him?"

"Wild ones look after themselves. They look after each other."

"How? What do they do?"

"They know which plants to eat if they have stomach troubles. I saw a wild one treat a sore on his back once."

"Yes?"

"He tore a branch from a sandalwood tree, stamped on it until the oil ran, and then he slapped it over his shoulder with his trunk. I wouldn't believe that if I hadn't seen it myself. They can manage. It was no accident when Shiva gave the god of wisdom an elephant head, Muthu!"

"No," said Muthu, laughing with him, and then—"But . . . if a wild elephant injured his trunk, then how would he manage?"

"They look after their trunks too well for that," said Rengan. "You've seen an elephant getting ready to charge, haven't you? What is the first thing he does? Rolls up his trunk and puts it in his mouth where it will be safe. An elephant with a damaged trunk would soon be a dead elephant!"

Muthu gave him a look that Rengan couldn't understand. He watched the boy walk away looking agitated. There was something wrong and it worried him. For several days he had known there was a thief around. He had been watching Palani very carefully ever since he had come back from the bazaar with an expensive pink shirt. Perhaps he should be watching Muthu as well.

Muthu had taken a whole kilo tin of the special ointment. Rengan had not noticed yet. He believed he had it in reserve because he always kept things in reserve in case of an emergency when a vet could not come. When he found out it would be too late. Everything was ready, in the hollow tree. His festival dhoti smeared thickly with the ointment and carefully folded. His mother would be angry about the dhoti but that was a minor problem. The big problem was how he was going to spread it over Ama's trunk. He would have to work it out in the morning when he got to the elephants' hideout. He knew how to get there now, it was easy. He would go along the river and surprise them, and then . . . well then . . . maybe Ganesha would help him after all. There was no sense in thinking about the things that might go wrong.

The day began badly at dawn. Palani was on to something. He kept edging towards Muthu as the two of them bathed Meenakshi, trying to get him out of earshot of the others. He succeeded.

"Where is the money?"

"Money?" Muthu said nervously. "What money?"

"From the things you have stolen. I know. From Rengan's stores. Even from your own mother you have stolen food!"

"Me? What are you saying?"

"I followed you. Sneaking out of the camp with a gunny bundle."

"You didn't," said Muthu wildly, giving himself away.

"Ha! You admit it!" Palani smirked with glee. "So where is the money? Well? Who did you sell the things to?"

Muthu concentrated on scrubbing Meenakshi's toe-nails. He was thinking desperately. If Palani thought he had been stealing to make money, then he hadn't followed him, and he could not know about the elephants. He could lie, it would give him time.

"I buried the money."

"If you don't dig it up and give it to me, I will tell everyone that you are the thief."

"I've forgotten where I buried it."

"Liar!" Palani twisted Muthu's arm behind his back and pushed him under the water behind the great, waiting bulk of Meenakshi where no one could see them. Muthu came up sobbing, retching, gasping for air. Palani told Meenakshi to get up. "Remembered now, Muthu?" he asked slimily.

"Yes," Muthu wrenched out, "but don't say anything!"

"Oh no, I won't say. It is a useful secret for me, cousin. Don't ever forget that I know it."

The rumour about a thief in their midst had swept through the camp like dysentery. No one escaped suspicion, and it was difficult for Muthu to get away. Finally in desperation he grabbed one of his sisters' saris off a bush where it was drying, wrapped up his parcel, put it on his head and walked boldly out of the camp. No one took any notice.

The river was more difficult to handle than he had expected, it kept changing. Sometimes it flowed idly through sparse jungle with grassy banks and flat rocks and he could walk along the banks. Then it changed, writhing like a snake and tunnelling itself through boulders and cliffs. He had to swim then, and had the rushing current not swept him along with its power he would have sunk under the weight of his bundle. It was two hours of twisting and turning before he saw the familiar cliff with the Ganesha shrine half-way up. One more bend, and then he would be swept into the bay with his elephants. And then? Would she understand, poor pain-wracked Ama, that he had come to help her? No. Was she really as weak as he imagined, much too weak to attack him? She couldn't use her trunk, but what could she do with her weight, with her hatred? He remembered Sita's shattered bangles, remembered Rengan . . . when a she-elephant goes bad . . . "it is a very terrible thing, worse than a male, many times worse."

He was crazy to have come, he knew that now the fear was exploding inside him. He drew on shreds of courage he had not had to use before to get himself round the last bend.

The bay was empty. The elephants had gone in the daytime. Now he was truly frightened.

6

Why? Had she gone into the jungle to die? No, she would have stayed near water for that. Had she sensed death coming and gone to find help for little Tumbu? Muthu dropped his life-saving bundle. He had to face it. Death was the easy way out. A voice—it was not his—put words into his mind.

There is a killer elephant roaming in the daytime, and only you, Muthu, know it.

He climbed up the gully and started to run back to warn the camp. A thorn lodged in his foot but he did not notice it until he reached the river bend where they bathed the elephants. He thrust his foot into the cooling, soothing water. He was being watched, the holy man's faded eyes dug into his back like two leeches. "What is wrong?"

"I . . . I have a thorn in my foot, Swami."

"Come, then." Muthu sat before him. He was trembling, sweating badly, feeling faint. He glanced at the old man's begging bowl.

"I . . . I have . . . nothing to give you . . ." he stuttered, ashamed.

"I don't ask for anything." Muthu jumped as the long tapered fingernails prodded his foot.

"You have been running on this thorn, it is hard to get out. To run on a thorn like this . . . you must have been frightened, very frightened."

"Yes . . . no, Swami . . . nothing, not really . . ."

"Nothing? Nothing as big as this . . . there is no good in it. There is evil." Muthu could not look at the eyes that saw the unseen. This was a new fear to him.

"I pray, Swami, I pray, truly. To Ganesha. He is a good god, isn't he? A wise god who helps you? Well, he hasn't helped me! He hasn't even answered my prayers!"

"Did you ask for too much? Ask for something that could not be?" The thorn came out, the ancient fingers rubbed the place where it had been. In the silence, Muthu felt the old man's holiness, it was something strong and gentle that reached for the truth.

"It isn't evil," Muthu said, knowing only that it was his voice that said the words, "but it is bad. It is not for me, it is for a friend that I ask help. He cannot help what he is doing. Does that make bad things better? Would Ganesha help such a one?"

The holy man's eyes stopped looking at eternity, suddenly he felt very close to earth. "Ganesha cannot *do* things for you. He gives you the wisdom to work them out for yourself. He takes obstacles out of your path so that you can see the way ahead. Now for you, and for your friend, has he shown you the way you have to go? Can you see the true path?"

"Yes," Muthu whispered miserably, "yes. I think so."

"You need courage to follow it, don't you?"

"Yes."

"Go then. Go."

The holy man blessed Muthu and watched him go. He sat for a while and meditated and then he picked up his staff and his begging bowl, and walked slowly towards the camp.

Muthu knew that the holy man was right. He did need courage, a different sort of courage now. The courage to betray Tumbu and Ama. But the wave of hostility that hit him when he walked into the camp washed it all away. People glared at him, some shouted, some spat. Then his mother. His mother! Screeching and crying so that the little children clutched at her sari. She pushed them aside.

"Muthu! How could you do such things! The shame! My son, a thief, a robber, a no-good! You should do this to us? Why? Why?"

Muthu backed away, shocked. His mother, when he needed her... Then it was Rengan, bearing down on him with a stick. Rengan too!

"Muthu, come here! Catch him, you stupid boys, bring him to me!"

Muthu ran down towards the river where he could hide. Palani was waiting, and grabbed his arm so he slewed round a bush.

"Palani?" Palani was pleased with himself, he was smiling nastily.

"Yes! *I* told them. They thought it was me, you see. Me who had been stealing . . . So I had to tell them, didn't I? Tell them it was you all the time. Tonight they will talk and make your punishment."

"No, no," said Muthu wretchedly, shaking his head slowly. Palani laughed. "Stealing from *elephants*, Muthu, you! And you thought you could be a mahout!"

Muthu's stone hit him on the forehead; by the time he had recovered from the shock and wiped the blood from his eyes Muthu was high up in the branches of a wild fig tree, well hidden, huddled like a lone monkey and weeping helplessly into an ants' nest. Look-out ants scurried out to investigate him, but soon decided that he was no threat to them.

The sounds from the camp—and they were unusually agitated through the day—did not break into his misery. It was a solid thing. But the whine of a jeep, labouring and thudding across the jungle, coming towards him . . . Vishnu-Vet? Could it be . . . the only person who could help Ama now?

"He went that way." Palani's voice was sullen. "Can I go now?"

"Yes, yes, go!" It was! Ganesha had listened to him after all. Muthu held his breath.

"Muthu? Muthu!" It was not the voice he had used to Palani. "Muthu, it is I, Vishnu-Vet, do you hear me? Call out, Muthu. I need your help." There was a testing silence. "I need your help. It is about a sick elephant." Muthu grasped a branch of the tree tensely and Vishnu saw it quiver.

"Come down. I can't shout to you up there." Muthu climbed down shakily.

"A sick elephant?" he said suspiciously, "then you would know, Rengan would know . . ."

"No one else knows about this elephant." Muthu bit his lip. It was all coming out now, boiling over. Should he let it? Must he follow the holy man's path? "Why would I know about it?"

Vishnu gave him a long hard stare. "Because you have been stealing from the elephants," he said evenly.

"I did it to get money!" Muthu said quickly.

"No. I don't think so. Rengan says you have been asking how wild elephants cure their injuries. The holy man came to the camp. He says you have a friend who is in very serious trouble. Well?"

"Yes . . . but it is a friend, I can't . . ."

"Muthu, this friend, I think it is a dangerous elephant." Muthu glared at the ground, his silence and then his tears gave him away.

"He . . . no, she is very ill," he sniffed, "you could make her well again."

"She? Muthu! Did you never *think*? This might be the killer elephant!"

"It is. But I know why! She has been shot . . . in her trunk . . . it is very, very bad . . . she can't get food . . . and now she has fever too . . . I took Rengan's ointment yesterday so that . . ." Vishnu's horrified expression checked him. "What's wrong?"

"You haven't been close to her?"

"Today I went, I was going to . . . but she had gone."

"Gone? When?" His words came out like shots and Muthu knew then that it was all over. He let out a cry that was hoarse and comfortless, like a wounded animal. "No! Not again, no, please, no!"

"The man is not dead, but he is old, Muthu. You understand now, don't you?"

"You are going to shoot her."

"Yes."

"You won't even try and make her better?"

"It is too late now, isn't it?"

"You don't know where to find her!" They stared at each other challengingly and then Muthu lowered his eyes. "You have your gun?"

"Yes, in the jeep, come. It is the kindest thing you can do for her now, Muthu." He meant it but his voice broke. To shoot an animal and end its pain was a part of his job and he could do it. But facing Muthu's courage, the terrible betrayal he had asked of him, there was no way to end that sort of pain.

"This isn't elephant country," Vishnu said as they turned towards the rocks. "How did you find her?"

"Ganesha brought me. There is an old shrine, I will show you." They stopped and Vishnu put his gun together. Muthu watched him, a last desperate plan brewing in his mind. "I will go and see if she has come back. Will you . . . will you wait until I call you?" He didn't think it would work. Vishnu was in charge now, he would say what would happen and what would not. Vishnu just nodded.

She had come back and was swaying piteously in the sun. Tumbu was a long way down the river, pulling up some weed and twisting it round his trunk. Why was he so far away? Was he keeping out of her way because she was dying? No, surely, he would have come to her knowing that. Then it was meant to be! Muthu leaned over the cliff.

"Ama, I'm sorry . . . but . . . listen to me! I am going to look after Tumbu for you. I want you to know that. No one knows about him, not even Vishnu-Vet. So no one will ever know that he . . . and you . . . he'll be all right Ama, I promise, promise you that!" He backed away quickly, and called out to Vishnu. He pointed to a rock where Vishnu would get a clear shot at Ama, but could not see Tumbu at all. They stood together on the rock looking down at her. Vishnu's gun smelled oily in the sun. He was shocked. Even for a vet, it was a terrible sight to see. How could the boy have lived with the animal's suffering, believed she could get well? "Go away, Muthu," he said sharply, "it will be very quick."

"Yes." Muthu swallowed nervously. "Will you wait . . . two, three minutes?" Vishnu nodded impatiently, he thought he understood. "Yes. Go."

Muthu went, scrambling like a wild thing, jumping from rock to rock, tumbling down the gully. He stopped briefly to tear off a long piece of creeper, skinning his hands, and was running again. The shot rang out, it whined echoingly through the cliffs. They moved together with the same impetus, boy and elephant. Tumbu was shuffling, panic-stricken, through the shallow water as Muthu's final dash down the cliff brought him into the bay. He hurled himself at Tumbu, looped the creeper over his neck and they moved in the same blind rush into the deeper waters where the current shook and buffeted them and then drew them together and sucked them into its main stream.

Vishnu let out a hiss of relief. His shot had gone straight into the elephant's brain, she had been mercifully dead before her tired legs crumpled and folded and she collapsed, like a great tent, on to the sand.

There was no answer when he called out to Muthu and he was glad. He hoped he had gone back to the camp because there were things to be done that would be unpleasant enough without the boy's anguish. It was eerie in the bay, alone with the dead elephant. Muthu had been right when he spoke about elephants lying down. He started composing his report in his mind as he examined the sad carcass. Small, Rengan had said the killer had been small. Grossly underweight, starving, severe stomach disorders, infections, fever . . . He must get the body burnt before the crows and kites and vultures started spreading disease. Age? He lifted the soft mouth flap and felt her teeth. The fourth great molar was hardly worn. He was shocked. She seemed old, but she was not more than twenty-five. His own age. Now the great misshapen trunk. It buzzed blackly with flies, maggots, maggots by the thousand wriggling, squirming, growing fat. Cause—peppered with shot, close range, probably a blunderbuss full of rusty nails . . . tetanus, she should have died of that before now. How had she survived so long? It seemed impossible she had had the strength to carry on. He cast around her sanctuary, noting how she had lived, what she had eaten . . . the sand was churned up near the water's edge, her footprints were clear.

Vishnu stared, suddenly: small prints. There had been other elephants with her? He checked carefully. Just one, a very small one. She had a calf? He went back to the body and heaved on a front leg to reveal her breasts. Yes, she had been feeding a calf. Not much, by the look of it, but there was still a trace of milk. He went back to the footprints. A young calf, he estimated, about four feet tall, a year old? There was no trace of it now, it had probably died, she would not have had the strength to take care of it. It was getting dark and he prepared to leave. He felt no hatred for the killer, only pity. No wonder, with a calf to protect, and wounds like those, she had hated people. He called down all the curses he could name on the person who had hurt her.

The news spread quickly. Relief that the killer had been taken from their midst caused celebrations in the camp and in the bazaar and Vishnu was a hero. He hated it, and got away as soon as he could. Muthu was the hero if anyone was. But Muthu was in disgrace, and Muthu was not there. Vishnu kept silent, Muthu was in enough trouble. As far as everyone else knew he was just a thief. But when his involvement with the elephant came out—if it did—what would he be then? A boy who had shielded an elephant he knew to be a killer, a boy who had known that the killer was out during the day and had not warned anyone. And if the old man died . . . the elephant people might try and understand, but the people from his village would not.

When Vishnu arrived in the camp before dawn to get a burning gang organised with Rengan he discovered that Muthu was still missing and a theory that had been building during a sleepless night became very possible. He hurried to the elephants' hiding place ahead of anyone else and searched it carefully. The sun had just come up and already the body was smelling and swelling alarmingly. He trampled over the marks the baby elephant had left and then climbed thoughtfully up the cliff to the shrine Muthu had pointed out. There were some dried up petals from flowers Muthu had left; the ants had taken away the grains of rice and the coconut. He thought about Muthu coming here alone, with the pressing weight of responsibility for the dying elephant and her calf on his shoulders. What a mess it all was. For that pitiful heap below on the sand he had sacrified everything. Now he was a thief, a liar, and maybe worse. Now he had cut himself off from his friends, his family, the camp and the elephants he had grown up with. The boy who only wanted to be a mahout! Because he had cared so much for one elephant, and believed he could help her, he had put himself in extreme danger and suffered unbelievable sorrow. Vishnu stared at the fat little god, and tried, through him, to get into Muthu's mind and work out what he might do next.

The baby elephant had not died, he knew that now. And the fact that it, and Muthu, were both missing was no coincidence. But where had they gone? Why had Muthu not brought it to the camp when he of all people would realise that it needed special care and feeding? Because he would not dare. The son or daughter of a killer, who had been with its mother when the violence happened? No, he would not dare bring such an elephant back. He would assume that everyone knew by now what he had done. He would not know that Vishnu had kept his secret to himself. For a Government vet, Vishnu realised he was in a very awkward position. He had to find Muthu.

The gang were coming to burn the elephant. Just

as they crashed down the gully, Vishnu saw a bundle on the shoreline. A small dhoti, covered thickly in ointment. "Muthu, you little fool," he whispered as he hurled it into the river.

7

The powerful river that had drawn Muthu and Tumbu into its depths poured them into a deep fast flowing gorge and finally abandoned them two miles downstream in white-flecked shallows. They floundered towards a small cove patterned with naked tree roots reaching down to the river. Muthu beached himself, gasping for breath. Tumbu stopped a few yards from the bank, resolutely facing the way he had come. They were both suffering from shock and exhaustion and now, after the wild excitement of their collision-charge out of the bay and into the river, came a very testing time. They had to face each other on land. Muthu sat still, dripping, waiting; only the muscles in his hand moved. Now he could see the elephant clearly for the first time as he stood stubbornly in the river, the water making white frills round his legs. Thin, far too thin, almost lanky, and aquiver with suspicion and confusion. Those were the immediate things. He had wiry strands of hair on his back like the outside of a coconut. His rubbery trunk was strong but a bit wavery, not quite under control yet. He used it now to test the different layers of the air. He was so beautiful that Muthu's heart ached for him yearning for his mother. He had to replace her, he had to be able to look after Tumbu. But what would Tumbu make of him? Their troubles had all begun with people, with a shot. Now there had been another shot and Muthu was the person. And those other people ... he had been there then. If Tumbu knocked him over and tried to knee him into the ground, Muthu wondered if he would be strong enough to throw him off. He was not afraid of being hurt, only of being hated.

He pulled tentatively on the creeper-rope now and then, and Tumbu resisted. It was an hour before he came out of the river, slowly, picking his feet up delicately. He stood at the far end of the cove, as far as he could get from Muthu and pressed himself against the tree roots. Muthu waited half an hour and then ... "Tumbu, Tumbu, Tumbu," he chanted, over and over. Tumbu flinched at the sound of a voice and Muthu kept his elephant chant up until the sun started to disappear.

"I have to get your food now," Muthu said in the same voice. Tumbu's eyes slid over him and then stared mournfully back up the river.

"Tumbu, you can't go back there. You couldn't swim against the current. Anyway ... she's not there any more. I am your mother now, and your father, and your Rengan and your Vishnu-Vet! Now

I am going to tie you to that big root over there, see?"

He moved very slowly and deliberately so that Tumbu could see exactly what he was doing and that he posed no threat. Then he pulled himself up on the tree roots and disappeared. He found he was in good mixed jungle and soon gathered a head-load of fresh bamboo and grasses which he threw down into the cove. He went back and found a mixture of roots and berries. When he returned to the cove it was almost dark and Tumbu had shown no interest in the food. That was a set-back if he wasn't going to eat, Muthu hadn't thought of that.

The elephant came up to about his armpit, so he thought he was probably a year and a half old, no more. At that age, camp calves were weaned so that their mothers could work, but they had special diets worked out by Vishnu-Vet and carefully weighed out by Rengan, according to their age and strength. But in the wild Muthu thought that baby elephants were not weaned for the several years they stayed close to their mothers. They ate other things of course, and their mothers taught them how to find their own food. What did Tumbu need? Muthu drifted into a worried sleep.

He woke once, because the night air was cold and he was shivering. There was a noise close by, a cracking, a rustling, a chomping. Muthu hugged himself with delight in the dark. Tumbu was eating! He was eating at last! The next time Muthu awoke it was getting close to dawn and there was a warm whiffling going on near his feet. He kept rock-still. Tumbu towered over him, he was mountainous in the half light. The tether must have come undone. He could feel the tip of Tumbu's trunk now, the rubbery lips investigating, the way Lakshmi had touched him when he was a baby. But this was not Lakshmi, he must remember that at all times. Tumbu was no camp elephant. The great feeling of tenderness that covered him like a warm blanket must not hide the fact that Tumbu was wild and must be treated with the greatest care.

Suddenly Tumbu got bored with Muthu's feet and he went down to the river, filled his trunk with water and squirted it noisily into his mouth. When Muthu stood up, he shuffled warily to his corner again.

"Tumbu, Tumbu, you came to *me* then, didn't you? You're nosey, hey? But I didn't hurt you, did I? We can trust each other, be friends? But I must tie you up again while I go and find you more food. I don't want to lose you now!"

When he came back the jungle was wide awake. A swarm of rock bees suddenly darkened the sky; one of their scouts buzzed into the cove and buzzed away again. Muthu was relieved, he didn't need bees today. There would be enough problems without bees. Tumbu had already started eating the grasses he had dropped into the cove. Muthu watched him with satisfaction as he took a big root and washed it carefully in the river before he stuffed it into his mouth. Good. He had remembered some of the things his mother had taught him. But when Muthu climbed down he backed away and refused to eat. He had to go away and wait until Tumbu started to eat again. Wasting precious time. And time was important. They had to get away from the river, it was too obvious. It was not safe. They would be searching for him now. "They" were becoming, in his mind, a big angry crowd, bigger every moment. Foresters and police, hostile elephant men, vengeful villagers, even Vishnu-Vet, even he would be the enemy now. They would all know what he had done and they would want to catch him, punish him. He did not mind for himself, it would just be unpleasant, maybe uncomfortable. But Tumbu, what would they do to Tumbu, the killer's son? He could not bear to think about it.

They trudged on all day until Muthu was feeling so tired and hot that he became head-achy and dizzy. His concentration flagged. Tumbu was following docilely now, at the furthest end of his tether. He was too docile, Muthu thought miserably, he should be more lively. But it was Tumbu who smelt the smoke first; he side-stepped, his little eyes rolled with alarm. Muthu was alarmed too, and angry because he had been caught off his guard. He should have seen signs, known there was a village ahead. It was quiet, more than quiet. It was the silence of people being deliberately quiet, waiting. An arrow hissed over Muthu's head and thudded into the ground behind him. He watched it quiver and laughed with relief. Of course there had been no sign of a village!

"Kurumbas, Tumbu!" He urged Tumbu to follow him and called ahead to show that he was harmless, just a boy with an elephant. They would not understand the words, but they should get the message. Rengan understood some of their language, he understood them, too, as few outsiders did. He had worked with them tracking game for Government reports, he always knew where to find them when he wanted fencing or thatching because their jungle craft was a perfect thing. Muthu had often watched them working and admired their quick fingers and their feeling for the wood, or palm, or bamboo they used. He liked their animal wildness too. One day they were there, the next day they had gone without a trace. Now he remembered something else that Rengan had told him. The Kurumbas knew a lot about elephants.

The whole tribe gathered round in their jungle enclosure when Muthu finally managed to coax Tumbu into their midst. Using a few words, and a lot of comic mime, Muthu explained that Tumbu belonged to him, that his mother had died—he mimed "stomach ache and poison"—and they laughed at his antics but got the point. They chattered and pointed to him, clearly saying, "What about you? Where is your family, your home?" His shirt and dhoti were dirty, torn, but they were not jungle made. Muthu mimed that he was wild like a monkey, he lived in the jungle. They understood his mime and laughed again but they did not believe him. A leathery old lady came up and pinched his cheek. She looked at him kindly and shouted shrill instructions to one of the huts. A man came and did the same thing to Tumbu, this time feeling his stomach, and opening his mouth. Muthu was shocked, and quickly tried to pretend that he was not. He had not attempted to touch Tumbu himself, he had not even tried to get close to him. But the man had done it and Tumbu had not even flinched.

A plantain leaf piled with steaming food—corn, sweet potatoes and some things Muthu did not recognise was brought for him. Some roots and fruits were brought for Tumbu. Muthu looked at them suspiciously and the man nodded and indicated that they were good for Tumbu. Muthu believed him, remembering what Rengan had said. There was a bucket, a sturdy bamboo cut off with a sloping bottom, full of buffalo milk for Tumbu too. Muthu grinned his thanks and retired with Tumbu to a corner of the Kurumbas' thorn fence.

He drifted off to sleep that night happy in the knowledge that he was safe, that he was well fed, and Tumbu had been properly looked after. Perhaps they could stay here . . . stay for ever . . . stay until they both felt stronger . . . stay, anyway . . .

The Kurumbas were active long before dawn. Muthu sensed it was not just their normal daily routine. There was an urgency about it and he saw two of the tribe leave their clearing with a definite purpose. He could tell, from the way they spoke and pointed, that they were not going about their normal work. This was different, special.

"They are not our friends, Tumbu," Muthu said sorrowfully. "Good people, but they know we have run away. They are going to tell someone about us. Rengan probably. So! That will take a day or so, we have time to get away."

They travelled, zig-zag style, through the jungle that day, barely stopping even when it was very hot. Muthu did not fool himself that he could hide his trail from the clever Kurumbas. But he could outwit anyone else. Two important things happened during the day. Tumbu and Muthu walked closer together, they even brushed against each other sometimes and once, to Muthu's real pleasure, Tumbu reached out his trunk towards him curiously, and allowed him to place his hand lightly on his neck. But the other thing was serious. Tumbu was not eating. He snatched occasionally at an overhanging branch, but immediately dropped it. He pulled up some grass, knocked it on his foot, and then dropped it and walked over it.

"Are you telling me something, Tumbu?" Muthu asked anxiously. "Since you had that milk last night ...you don't want to eat grown-up things, is that it?" He lay down in the shade for a rest, worrying about it. Did Tumbu really *need* milk? Would he die because he had been weaned suddenly? He was certainly very thin. If Tumbu needed milk then he had to have it and that meant going back to the camp. Rengan would give him milk and all the right food he needed. And vitamins, worm pills. Vishnu-Vet would come and check him all over. Maybe he would find he had caught something from his mother. What? Something inside him that did not show yet? His longing for the security of the camp was as great as his dread of going back to it. How could he decide what was best for Tumbu? He had to decide. Every elephant man knew that his elephant's needs came before his own, no matter what happened. But if he saved Tumbu, he might lose him too.

Wild elephants, was that an answer? Tumbu was still wild. A herd would take him in, find him an auntie to care for him, give him her milk. They did that in the wild, he knew. They would not even mind that Tumbu had been with him, herd instincts were strong enough for that. Muthu made up his mind, they would go on that day, and if they found a wild herd ... well, good. Tumbu would go off and join them and that would be all right for Tumbu. Muthu would be alone then, that was something he would have to deal with when the time came. He did not want to think about it yet.

They came to a heavy teak plantation, the jungle floor crinkly with brown leaves. Tumbu was cautious, he investigated this new ground carefully before he would walk on it. But he was not cautious for long and neither was Muthu. Suddenly the ground disappeared from beneath their feet and they were falling, a tangle of thick grey limbs and thin brown ones, in an assortment of human shouts and elephant squeals. They thudded to the bottom of a deep pit. Muthu thought, dazedly, that something should hurt somewhere, but it didn't. Not then. Above there was a small patch of vivid blue sky broken by soaring tree branches. It was getting darker, the patch of blue was going round, making him feel sick and dizzy. And then it had gone, it was totally dark and Muthu knew nothing, felt nothing.

Vishnu's map of the game reserve was falling apart at the creases. He flattened it out on the bonnet of the jeep and stared helplessly at the shaded bits—so many of them now—where he had searched for Muthu. He could barely face Muthu's distraught parents any more. His father and the faithful, uncomplaining Lakshmi set off each dawn, and dragged themselves back, tired, defeated, in the evening.

Rengan's shadow fell across the map, silently he stabbed it with a leathery finger.

"There?" said Vishnu in surprise. It was a teak area, brown and dry under the trees, not lush and green, not the sort of place a boy would take a young elephant.

"Kurumbas came," Rengan muttered secretively,

"wanted to trade a young elephant with us." Vishnu's face lit with hope. The two men exchanged a long, trusting look. There was no need to speak about the secret they now shared.

"I will go now," Vishnu said. "How close can I take the jeep?"

"Some miles," said Rengan vaguely. "I will send elephants and mahouts after you. The Kurumbas will say nothing, I gave them some of our stores."

"Good. I'll see that is accounted for." Rengan grunted and watched him go.

Light, dark, heat, cold, pain and nothingness. These things came, they went, they got muddled together. There were clear moments too that Muthu was to remember afterwards. The deep brown smell of dank earth. Tree roots standing out like twisted white snakes. Something grey, warm and scratchy that whimpered for food.

"Tumbu, be quiet, I can't help you. My head hurts . . . I can't move . . . Lie down and go to sleep, can't you? Leave me alone."

"*No! Tumbu, no, don't lie down! You mustn't lie down!*"

Who said that? Muthu tried to pull himself up on a tree root, the dank earth trickled over his shoulders. He could see Tumbu properly now, leaning weakly against the side of the pit, his eyes pleading—get us out of here, do something, you're supposed to be looking after me.

"I promised your mother," said Muthu weakly, "but we're in a pit, Tumbu . . . it's an old one, so no one will come . . ." He tried again to get up and the pit started to go round. It was getting dark again, there was just a greyness, it was getting bigger, Tumbu was growing and filling the pit, he would be suffocated. Big white tusks, gleaming . . . no, not tusks, tree roots. Tumbu, getting smaller, shrinking against the side of the pit, going away . . .

"No! No, Tumbu, don't go away . . . Tumbu, don't lie down, don't lie down . . ."

"Lie down. Lie down, there's a good boy." The voice was peculiar, it came from a very long way away.

"No, Tumby, *don't* lie down."

"*You* lie down, child. Who is this Tumby fellow? Tumby, Tumby, always Tumby?"

Then another voice, much closer this time. His mother was in the pit too?

"Muthu, drink this. Why did you run away? Muthu, you hear me? He doesn't, he still doesn't hear me."

"Come away now, the doctor is here."

"Please, doctor, do something, he is my eldest son, he mustn't die!"

Then another voice broke into his consciousness.

"It's me, Vishnu-Vet, remember? Muthu, listen, I have your Tumbu, he is in the camp and he is getting better. Tumbu will live, and so must you!"

Perhaps he was close to the gods. It was dreamy,

like heaven, floating down the river with his elephant at his side. A bright hoopoe swooped over their heads, a pig squealed to her mate on the bank. Kurumbas! An arrow in the ground, quivering, spikey jungle, falling, falling, dank earth, tree roots. "Where's Tumbu?" Soft hands touched him, wiped his face. The woman with the strange voice came into focus. She had a cloth over her head like a Moplah woman but she was a funny colour. Like a tourist. Was he at Theppakkadu now then? Where the tourists sometimes came for elephant rides?

"I am a nurse, a nun," she said, confusing him. His mother was there suddenly, laughing and crying at once and touching him as if he had just come back from a distant place and she could not quite believe it. He was lying on a veranda shaded by bougainvillea, the brilliant purple of the flowers hurt his eyes. There were other people lying on bedding rolls too. It was a puzzling place.

"Where's Tumbu?" His mother and the nun looked blank. What was happening, had they all gone funny while he was away?

"Tumbu," he said firmly, "my elephant. There was a hole, in the jungle, I thought he would lie down and die . . . He is just a baby, he was sick."

"You were sicker, child," said the nun reprovingly.

"He did die, he *did*!"

"Hush, Muthu! No, he is in the camp. Rengan and Vishnu-Vet are looking after him like a raja. Who fell in the pit first, you or the elephant? Such bruises you had, Muthu! I think the elephant fell on you!"

"He does not remember," said the nun, "it is not surprising after such a fever."

"I do remember," said Muthu slowly, "we both fell together. He was with me, you see . . ."

"No, no, Muthu, you are confused," said his mother, laughing. "It was a wild elephant, not a camp one. It could not have been with you." Muthu drifted off into sleep again, it was easier than trying to think.

Vishnu came another day when Muthu was stronger. His mother salaamed shyly and went away.

"Is it true?" asked Muthu eagerly. "Tumbu is in the camp, he is well?"

"He is weak, like you, but getting stronger all the time."

"What does he do? Is he settling down?"

"Yes, very well. He eats most of the time, yesterday he started to play. He likes the other new elephant, remember? He fell in a pit too, maybe that is why they seem to understand each other so well. And Meenakshi is his auntie now, she is always close to him, making a fuss of him! She looks after him like . . . like his real mother would." There was a silence full of unsaid things.

"How did you find us?" said Muthu quickly.

"The Kurumbas tracked you, otherwise . . . you would not have been found. There are too many pits, the Range Officer is worried about them, he is having an investigation. I have to write a report about this elephant you ... found." Muthu was ready for the question.

"I found him trapped in the pit," he lied smoothly, "and so I tried to reach down ... and I fell. So, we were both trapped, and the little elephant ... I called him Tumbu, he was sick. I was afraid he would lie down, like Meenakshi when she was sick, but ..." Vishnu's disbelieving stare stopped him.

"You don't believe me," he said, sounding injured.

"His mother wouldn't have left him in a pit. She would have gone and found some other elephants to help her get him out."

"Yes! I thought of that. Maybe he had run off ... or she was ill ... maybe she fell into another pit?" It was useless. He should have known better than to try and fool someone like Vishnu.

"The Kurumbas told you," he said, resigned. Vishnu shook his head.

"They didn't have to tell me, I knew. After I shot the mother, I knew then."

"They won't keep him, then. Because he is a bad one's son, he will be bad too. That is what they will all say—but it isn't true! He is a good elephant, a gentle elephant, I know he is!"

"Shh! No one knows where he came from. It will be as you said. You found him, abandoned in a pit. He will stay and be trained in your camp."

Muthu lay back, exhausted, but warmed with happiness. It was all too good to be true. So good it couldn't be true. The warmth was not there any more. He opened his eyes. Vishnu was gazing uneasily out into the compound of the little mission hospital.

"If Tumbu stays," Muthu said very slowly, "he will have to have a mahout." Vishnu got up to go. "Yes," he said abruptly.

"No!" It came out like a squeal. "Not Palani, please, no, not Palani!"

8

"Why don't you go and see Ramu?"

"Tumbu," said Muthu automatically. "I don't want to see him. He is Palani's elephant."

"Of course he is Palani's elephant. You always knew Palani would be next." Muthu turned away. It was joyless being back in the camp. He had never realised before how strong the elephants' presence was, their noises and smells would not go away. His mother would not leave him alone.

"Oh, Muthu," she said, trying to be kind, "you must have *known* it could not be your elephant. How could you think otherwise?"

"I found him. He *was* mine. He knows he's mine."

His mother started to rub coconut oil into his legs which were still stiff from his accident. She wished she could rub his mind and ease away the pain there, the grief and bitterness about the little elephant which she could not understand. Everything should be normal again after the weeks of drama and worry over Muthu. But they were not normal, there was something left over. The camp gossip about Muthu being a thief had ended when she came back with him from the hospital. Vishnu and Rengan had stopped it somehow. She had not questioned how, it was enough that her son was cleared and everyone welcomed him back. But there was a mystery about the elephant, there were deep and unknown things that made him cry out in the night. She finished rubbing his legs and patted his head. "Get up, Muthu. It is not good for you to lie about all the time in the hut."

Palani had no sympathy. He came and squatted at the entrance to the hut. "So," he said lightly, "Muthu is better but he won't *be* better. That isn't very grown up, is it? Well?"

"Go away."

"I'm going. There is a lot of work to do now I have my elephant to look after. He's called Ramu, did you know?" Palani waited for Muthu to lose his temper but nothing happened. Muthu's anger was too deep for that, there was nothing on the surface.

"I have to go to the bazaar," said Palani disappointed. "Not for me, you understand, for Rengan. So get up and do some work."

Muthu waited until Palani would have left the camp, and then he got up. He hesitated at the entrance. What if Tumbu did not remember him? It might be better not to put it to the test. He could see him now across the camp, there was no turning back. He was tethered to a tree by his back leg. He had a pile of bamboo and grass in front of him and he was sorting through it choosing the bits he liked best. He looked much better, Muthu thought, still thin but not starving-thin; livelier. He was so beautiful that Muthu felt choked to see him. "Tumbu?" he called nervously. The little elephant stood absolutely still. Grass hung from both sides of his mouth. His little eyes swivelled short-sightedly, his trunk layered the air. With a squeal of recognition he stumbled to the end of his tether.

Rengan watched them together, he saw them arm-and-trunk-wrestling. Playing together, being together, so close, so happy together that his heart sank because he had to end it. Now, before it was too late. If it wasn't already too late.

Muthu looked up proudly. "He's a fine elephant, isn't he, Rengan? Hey, Tumbu, you're the best. You think he'll be a tusker, Rengan?"

"Too soon to tell," said Rengan gruffly. "Call him Ramu. That's his name." Muthu did not like Rengan's tone. He stopped playing with Tumbu.

"What's wrong?"

"He is not your elephant."

"I *know*!" Muthu said rudely, and then stared contritely at the ground. Tumbu came and nuzzled him with his trunk, wondering why the games had stopped. "Push him away from you," Rengan said firmly.

"No! Rengan, *no!*"

"Yes. Do as I say, Muthu, this is Palani's elephant. He is in training."

"He is too young to be in training!"

"He has to learn about being with people."

"I taught him that . . ."

"He has much to learn." Rengan paused, it was hurting him having to hurt Muthu. "He has much to forget." Muthu moved away from Tumbu, staring suspiciously at Rengan. What was he saying, what did he know? Why didn't he say what he knew? Did he know about the blunderbuss packed with rusty nails, the bang, the rotting trunk . . . grey baggy knees bending, leaning, a switch of sari, a twist of dhoti . . . creak, grunt, squash . . . little evil, hating eyes . . . *and the little one, he was there when it happened!* The old man had died, too. You could have stopped it, Muthu, you knew! *Tumbu was there that time, too.* Rengan did not say any of these things. He just hinted that he knew them. He was touching the raw edges, to see if Muthu would cry out in pain.

"Do elephants . . . ever forget?"

Rengan smiled sadly. "This one has to forget and you have to help him."

"How?"

"You know how."

"By keeping away from him, you mean? So that he forgets me?"

"If you want him to have a chance, Muthu, yes. You can help him start again. He has to know his master, his mahout. It isn't fair to confuse him."

Muthu walked away, hunched over his despair.

Rengan wanted to go after him, to calm him as he would an injured elephant. But he had to grow up, didn't he? Like Ramu.

Two jeeps buzzed into the camp that evening with a lot of important people. There was a flurry of excitement. *Two* jeeps! The Range Officer, and a Government engineer who built grand things in far-away places. They all had assistants and assistant assistants and lots of papers. They showed the elephant men maps and photographs and everyone gathered round as keenly as if it had been a travelling filmshow. Muthu hovered curiously on the edge of the crowd. It was a dam project, a big one, far away in hill country. There was a lot of work to be done, jungle clearing, bridge and road building. Materials and machinery had to be hauled to the site. Important work, work that only trained elephants with good mahouts and kavadis could do.

The elephant men were smug. There were machines now, they had heard, that could do anything. So wasn't it strange that when it came to real work, they needed elephants? The engineer tried, very seriously, to explain and the elephant men laughed amongst themselves.

But after the jeeps buzzed off again they thought of all the reasons why they should not be the ones to go.

"It is a long way, six days' journey, more. What if the monsoon comes early?"

"What about our families? How will they live?"

"Eight elephants, eight mahouts, eight kavadis . . . and then there must be boys for grass cutting, helping . . . what will happen here?"

"It will not be three months, it will be six months at least. You know how these things are."

It was not really for the mahouts to decide. However much they believed that the elephants were theirs alone to control, they really belonged to the Indian Government and each one cost it a hundred rupees a day. They would go if they were told to go. Muthu saw Rengan talking earnestly to his father, and he had a hunch they were talking about him. He was right. "Go," said Rengan, "and take the boy. It is the best thing that could happen, get him right away from here before things get any worse." His father agreed. "Yes, you're right, Rengan," he was saying, "but what will his mother say?"

Muthu was angry. Never mind what his mother might say. What about him? He hadn't even been consulted! Well, he wouldn't go and that was that. If they thought they could separate him from Tumbu this way they were wrong. They would find that out! He couldn't go anyway. What if Palani and Tumbu didn't get on together? He wouldn't blame Tumbu for that, but other people would. What if Palani didn't understand that Tumbu was different from other elephants, and Tumbu hated him, what if—?

Muthu was not spying on Palani and Tumbu, he just happened to come across them in the river, fooling about, playing together, happy together. Palani was not putting on a show to make Muthu jealous this time. It was real. He could get along with Tumbu. Well, fine, good. Just what Rengan wanted. Tumbu had his chance to start all over again, good for Tumbu, as long as he was happy—the traitor. Little grey traitor, Muthu thought miserably, after all I did for you, you can have fun with somebody else—even be happy with Palani!

He decided that he wanted to go away now, far away, because staying in the camp would be unbearable.

"Ramu will miss you," said Rengan as they prepared to leave. He meant to be kind, to keep the link open for Muthu even though he was breaking it. Muthu did not see that.

"Ha! Tumbu is happy enough without me! Well, he will see I can forget, too."

"Elephants forget?"

"This one does. Oh yes, this is a very special elephant. He forgets very quickly." Muthu spoke so savagely that Rengan winced.

Palani would be wild as a tiger with envy when the letters arrived, Muthu thought with glee. He could picture him sitting there back at the camp when they were read out. Each month-end the letter-writer came to the mahouts' lines at the dam site and wrote down their news to send to the camp with the money they had earned. Most of the news was about the elephants. How they had managed the eight-day journey and coped with the hills and the colder weather. How important they were at the dam, how important it was to be a mahout or a kavadi, or even a grass cutter, amongst people who had never seen elephants working before. The engineers were impressed to see how they cleared the jungle, pushing down huge trees with their great foreheads, dragging one-ton loads, balancing log piles to the smallest fraction of an ounce, using their brains and their memories to move bulky machinery over difficult terrain. Elephants were heroes and heroines, it was good to be with them!

"Tell my mother," Muthu had said, meaning tell Palani too—"that we live in huts made of wood and stone and there is electric for lights and water coming in pipes almost to our doors. Tell her I have made some of the money we send, I am hooking logs for my father and Lakshmi now. Tell her I have lessons after work twice each week so I shall come back clever. And tell her we have film shows, not the ones that keep breaking down, these are called videos, and there is a hospital and a temple for us and a mosque for the Moslems and another temple for the Christians like the nun we met."

When the time came to go back nearly a year had passed because they had been held back by the monsoon and landslides in the hills. It was a wild, frightening monsoon in the hills and Muthu's father, who was the headman, would not let the elephants travel. Muthu was taller now, heavier, and wiser. He was not a jungle child to be pushed around any more.

The camp was decorated with flowers and bamboo welcome arches and there were garlands for everyone. A drum and reed pipe band played to celebrate the elephants' homecoming and the women all wore their brightest saris and flowers in their hair. The excited chattering, shouting of the people mingled with the happy grunting and occasional trumpeting of the elephants. Muthu scanned the eager faces, picked out his own family and Rengan and then looked for Tumbu. The elephants were dressed up too, and decorated with coloured powder. Tumbu, being the smallest, was at the end of the line, trying to eat his garland. He stopped when Lakshmi knelt to let her riders climb down and his trunk wavered, questing.

"Tumbu!" Muthu had not meant to call out. The sight of the elephant—grown upward, outward and handsome beyond belief—was overwhelming.

"Ramu!" Palani snarled furiously. He was trying to hold his body against Tumbu to keep him back, but he ignored Palani and stumbled towards Muthu, his trunk out in a straight line. Palani skidded along behind in the orange dust. People stopped greeting each other and started laughing delightedly as the comic scene was played out. An elephant—and a baby like that—disobeying his kavadi was not normally funny. But no one liked Palani very much and there had been rumours that little Ramu didn't either and everyone wondered why. Ramu stopped when he reached Muthu, investigated him curiously with his trunk to find out where he had been and then with a happy rumbling noise he leant his head against Muthu and they stood there together as if they were alone.

"Take him away, Muthu," hissed Palani, "you make a fool of me." Muthu pushed against Tumbu, who just rumbled again. "You take him," Muthu said, "he's yours."

"I can't. You know he won't come. Walk over to my place with me." Muthu could have made it worse. Walked in the opposite direction, taking Tumbu with him. But he didn't want to spoil the day, even for Palani. He walked back to Palani's place in the line. Palani put his arm round his shoulders and talked loudly. No one was fooled. Rengan was worried.

Now that he was back, Muthu could not remember how he had enjoyed the dam site so much. Here it was so lush: steamy jungle, waving bamboo, red earth. No straight lines, harsh electric lights or unfriendly concrete beneath his feet. No more strangers who didn't know about elephants. And Tumbu. His mother had prepared special food for them, and there was a wide plantain leaf spread with bananas and coconuts and sugar cane for Lakshmi. It was good to be back, good to see his mother so pleased to have them back. She showed them proudly the things she had bought with the money they had sent, new cooking pots, a mat for the floor, clothes for the smallest children. And something else, a new image with the household gods.

"Ganesha!" said Muthu. "Mother, you have a Ganesha now!"

"Not I—Vishnu-Vet brought it before he went away! Oh, but we were so overcome, so important he is becoming and he came *here*! Everyone looked and asked, I can tell you!"

"Vishnu-Vet has gone away? Where?"

"To Bombay, in an aeroplane! There is a new vet now."

It was two days before Muthu could talk to Rengan on his own. He had an uneasy feeling that the old man was avoiding him.

"Well, Muthu," he said when he was finally trapped, "I hear you worked well at the dam."

"Yes," said Muthu, pleased, "but I am glad to be back. Tum . . . the one you call Ramu, he has grown."

"You thought he would get smaller?" Rengan smiled, distantly.

"He remembered me," Muthu said hesitantly.

"I saw what happened. It has not been easy for Palani, that elephant has a mind of his own. After you left . . . he used to break away. He found your hut, not once, several times I heard your mother calling to Palani that his elephant would break down her hut."

"He did that? Looking for me?" Muthu said delightedly, and then he saw that Rengan looked anything but delighted. "I can't help it, Rengan, I never forgot him either, not for one day." He paused and looked at Rengan. "There's something wrong? Something wrong with Tumbu?"

"Yes. You have to know this Muthu, he may not make a working elephant."

"*Why?*"

"He gets moody, strange. He does not have the bond with people he should have by now, it is nearly a year . . ."

"Because he was wild, not camp-born!"

"Muthu, we used to have many wild elephants trained in the camps. Even a grown wild elephant sheds its wild nature after six weeks. But not this one, and he is young. He is holding back, keeping his wildness. Maybe it is because he can never learn to trust people that he will not obey them, will not let them master him."

"He trusts me."

"You are not his mahout."

"He hates Palani! He will never obey Palani!"

"That is unfair, Muthu."

"It's true! He doesn't hate me, I could train him, I know I could!"

Rengan nearly hit him then, but he got up instead and strode away trying to hold his anger. He was angry with Muthu because he thought he might be right, he probably could handle the elephant. But he was more angry with himself because he was head elephant man and he could not change the system even when it was wrong.

Muthu ran after him. "Rengan! If he can't be a camp elephant . . . then . . . Rengan, he can't go back to the jungle, not now." Rengan stopped.

"No. They are sending inspectors to assess him. The new vet thinks he will be dangerous when he gets bigger."

"The new vet! What do *you* say?"

"I cannot take the risk, Muthu. Understand that, you must. If he cannot stay here, they will take him to the zoo at Mysore." Rengan strode on again and Muthu let him go. "No," he said decisively, "not that. Not for Tumbu. Not a city, he would die. I would run wild with him before that happened."

Rengan was right about Palani and Tumbu, but he was wrong really, Muthu reflected, as he watched them training together in a clearing. Weeks, that's all you needed to teach a young elephant to sit, stand, do simple movements. Tumbu wasn't stupid, he knew what to do. He just didn't want to obey Palani. He waited until the last moment, until Palani was about to lose his temper, before he did. It was a distrustful and unhappy relationship. Palani picked up a chain attached to a rope. "Well, stupid, can you put that round this tree trunk?" Muthu stiffened. Tumbu took the rope end in his trunk, he looked at the tree trunk, moved the chain with one foot. Palani hit Tumbu's trunk with a bamboo cane. "Not that way, you dumb brute, *this* way!" Tumbu backed away edgily, the chain linked back untidily on itself and Tumbu dropped the rope end and looked at Palani with sly defiance.

"No, Tumbu," Muthu whispered, shocked, "you're not like that, you're not."

Palani had had enough. "Idiot face!" he snarled. "You need another beating, don't you. Or maybe I'll tie you up again away from your food. Remember that, do you?"

Tumbu evidently did remember. He tucked his trunk carefully to one side and walked very deliberately towards Palani. Palani retreated nervously, he was not shocked as Muthu was shocked, it must have happened before.

"Don't do that, you vicious brute. Keep away. Keep away I tell you, you no-good son of a killer!"

"Muthu, stop coming to me with your tales. Don't tell *me* how to run this camp, it is not your business."

"Being cruel to an elephant is anyone's business," blurted Muthu, he no longer cared if he was disrespectful to Rengan. "Making an elephant dangerous, whose business is that? Teaching a left-sided elephant to be right-sided, is that what a mahout should do?" He stared defiantly at Rengan and then he ran away, ashamed of the way he had spoken.

Rengan was only annoyed with himself. If Muthu

was right—and vaguely remembered events over the past year suggested he was—then he should have noticed. Was he getting old? Why had he not watched Palani more closely? He was lying sulkily in the shade when Rengan got to the clearing. Out of the elephant's reach, Rengan noted at once, and Tumbu was looking at him meanly.

"What's wrong with your elephant?" Palani jumped up, startled.

"He's in a vicious mood. Don't go near him. *Don't*, Rengan!"

Rengan glared scornfully at Palani and went up to Tumbu, talking gently. After a few minutes he told him to turn and walk with him. Tumbu did, slowly, watching him anxiously to see if he was doing the right thing.

"Good," said Rengan, "very good." He picked up the rope and chain and held it out to him. He gave the command and Tumbu took the rope end in his trunk and put it cautiously in his mouth. "Good," said Rengan again. "Now walk with it, drag the chain." Tumbu started to walk and then stopped. He took the rope out of his mouth and turned it round. Now when he walked the chain came across in front of him. He stopped, confused.

"Does he always do that?"

"Do what?"

"Turn the rope, didn't you see? Is he right-sided or left-sided?"

"How would I know?"

"You would know because he is your elephant!" Rengan was shouting now. "You would know a simple thing like that! What have you *done* to him? Here, show me how he works with you."

"I'm not coming near the brute. He's dangerous, he came straight at me just now."

"Dangerous? He is dangerous with me? Well, Palani, any time now they are coming to assess this fellow. If he fails he will be sent away, do you understand that? We have never failed with an elephant in this camp, it will be a disgrace."

"I can't help it. He's got a killer instinct, you can tell. He should never have come."

"Vishnu-Vet did not say that when he brought him here," said Rengan carefully, wondering what Palani knew.

"Vishnu-Vet is not here now though, is he? The new vet knows this one has madness in his head. It's not my fault he's no good."

"You're afraid of him. A mahout afraid of his elephant!"

"No!"

"Show me, then."

Muthu had found Meenakshi down by the river and he was telling her all about Tumbu's problems because she had made herself Tumbu's auntie and she loved him too. She was listening, wisely, and then she was suddenly alert and listening to something else. Distant panicky shouts; Muthu stiffened.

A child came tumbling down the bank. "Rengan says to come," he gasped, "come quickly."

"Why?"

"Ramu ... he is killing Palani against a tree!"

Muthu stumbled into the clearing, knotted with dread. A small crowd had gathered to see the drama and someone, Palani's mother perhaps, screamed hysterically. Muthu started to laugh.

"Stop that!" said Rengan. "Talk to him, Muthu, but don't go close."

Tumbu had broken his tether and Rengan was trying to tie the working rope to his back leg and pull him away at the same time. But Tumbu would not move. He had got Palani wedged against a tree with his head. Muthu had never seen anyone so frightened, Palani's eyes rolled wildly and he mouthed screams for help that wouldn't come out.

Muthu went straight to Tumbu and tapped him playfully on the head.

"Now then, Tumby, what is this naughty thing you are doing? Trying to frighten poor Palani, are you?" Tumbu lifted his head and Palani slid to the ground, groaning. "Come away now," said Muthu, leading the elephant by his ear. Tumbu made a low chirruping noise and as he turned, Rengan saw the mischief in his eyes. He threw the rope aside and wiped his face to hide a grin that was as much relief as amusement. Palani groaned again.

"Get up," said Rengan roughly.

"I can't. My back is broken, my ribs are crushed..."

"Only your pride is hurt. Get up and see to your elephant."

"Rengan, you saw! He tried to kill me. Now you know how dangerous he is. You'll have to get rid of him. I told you he was a killer. Where is he now?" Palani sat up and looked round. He saw Rengan watching Muthu and Tumbu playing with a piece of bamboo. Saw the crowd drifting away, talking about him, looking back with broad grins.

"Muthu! Always *Muthu*! He uses magic, bad magic. There is a demon in that elephant and Muthu can talk to it. How can I be expected to work against evil magic? I can't speak to demons!"

There was an amazed silence at Palani's outburst and then the noise of an approaching jeep broke into it. People were shouting for Rengan. He sighed. "Now of all times, they have come to assess your elephant, Palani."

"Good. The sooner they take him away the better. Muthu will have to take him back to the camp. Don't ask me to go near him."

Palani went off in the direction of the bazaar and Rengan hurried back to meet the jeep. Muthu was alone with Tumbu. Tumbu was still trying to wrestle with the piece of bamboo.

"Stop now," said Muthu, "be serious for once, can't you? This is your whole future, it will be decided in the next few minutes ... what are we to do? Tumbu, you can't go to a zoo, not to a city. I've heard about them and you wouldn't like it. You belong here. So? Shall we run away again, back to the jungle? We weren't very good at it last time. We can't stay wild forever . . . listen, they are calling for you. What will they think of an elephant who frightens his mahout away . . . the worst, the very worst. Oh, Tumbu!"

They couldn't take him away! Not in a jeep. Someone would have to walk him to Theppakkadu, they would load him onto a lorry from there . . . so there was time, time to plan an escape. He smoothed his shirt and tied his dhoti neatly. "Come, Tumbu."

Rengan was talking to two men. The Range Officer was one and the other . . . Vishnu-Vet in strange new clothes! Vishnu! What would this mean? Surely *he* could not send Tumbu to a zoo . . . yes, he could, he knew too much about his past . . . had even known his mother. Muthu stopped a little distance from the men and waited dutifully with Tumbu.

"I don't know what trouble this is," Rengan was saying. "It must be a mistake, there has been no trouble with this one."

"It was reported . . . never mind, let's see what he's like. Is that the kavadi? I thought . . ."

"The rascals all look the same to me," said Rengan, laughing casually. "Muthu, bring him here." Vishnu did not remember him? When Muthu turned to smile a welcome to him he just frowned and turned away. The Range Officer explained to him that this was Mr Vishnuswamy, the Chief Veterinary Officer in charge of all the elephants in the State. Muthu just nodded, feeling confused. He went on being confused. Rengan made him put Tumbu through his paces, which he did almost perfectly. Then they waited while the men talked and wrote things down on papers. Muthu's neck ached with the tension. What were they doing, why did they write things down about Tumbu if he was going away? Could it . . . could it possibly mean . . . he was staying after all? It seemed unfair that Muthu had had to do Palani's work, he would get the credit for it in the end. They would say what a fine kavadi Palani was to train an elephant so well! But Tumbu would not go to a zoo. Vishnu called him over at last, but he was still a stranger.

"This is his book," he explained. "You see, I have put his age, his weight, height . . . all the details about him."

"Yes," said Muthu, thinking, tell Palani, not me.

"What is your name?"

"My name?" Muthu stared at him questioningly, why was he being so stupid? Suddenly Vishnu smiled and gave a little nod that said there was a secret going on. Muthu grinned back, relieved.

"Muthuswamy, sir," he said, playing along.

Vishnu wrote it down. "Do you understand," he said solemnly, "what a great responsibility an elephant is? He has many needs, and his needs must always come before the needs of his kavadi and mahout. He must be healthy and happy if he is to have a good working life. He must be cared for at all times, not just today or next year, but for the rest of his life. For the rest of both your lives together. All right, Muthuswamy, stop dreaming, put your thumb in here."

"What? There?" Muthu came out of his daydream. Vishnu was patiently holding out the blue tin to him.

"Come on! We need your thumb print on his record book!" Muthu pressed his thumb on the blue pad.

"My thumb print?" he said stupidly, forgetting he had learnt to write his name. Suddenly he saw his father watching him. Had he been there all the time? He had tears of pride in his eyes.

"Yes, your thumb print," said Vishnu laughing, "he's your elephant, isn't he?"